Walking Through the Psalms

A Journey of Truth, Trust, and Praise

Russell Vance McFall

This book is a personal reflection on Scripture and spiritual truth. It is not intended to function as a formal commentary or academic theological work.

Published by **Ordained Path Books**
For permissions or inquiries, contact: ordainedpathbooks@gmail.com

Cover illustration and interior artwork generated by AI under the direction of the author.

First Edition

Scripture Note

"Your word is a lamp to my feet
And a light to my path."
—Psalm 119:105 (NASB)

Ordained Path Books is dedicated to stories and reflections that express timeless truth, courage, and the quiet strength of faith—guided by purpose and written to encourage the next generation.

ISBN (Paperback): 978-1-972724-14-9

Printed in the United States of America.
Version 1.00 — April 2026

Dedication

To my children—
These are the truths I would share with you,
one step at a time.

Foreword

This book is not a commentary.

It is not a study guide, and it is not meant to explain every detail found in the Psalms.

It is simply a collection of truths.

Truths I have come to understand over time—through Scripture, through life, and through the steady process of learning to walk with God. These are the kinds of things I would sit down and share with my own children, not all at once, but piece by piece, as life unfolds.

The Book of Psalms has a unique way of speaking to every part of life.

It speaks when things are clear.
It speaks when things are uncertain.
It speaks in moments of joy, and it speaks just as clearly in moments of difficulty.

There is honesty in the Psalms that is not forced. Questions are asked. Burdens are expressed. Trust is learned. And through it all, one thing remains steady:

God does not change.

This book is built around that truth.

Each reflection focuses on a small portion of Scripture—not to limit what is there, but to allow it to be considered more carefully. The goal is not to move quickly, but to think clearly. To take what God has said and allow it to settle, one truth at a time.

The sections follow a simple path.

We begin by considering who God is.
Then we look at how we walk with Him.
We face what happens when life becomes difficult.
We learn what it means to trust Him.
We respond with praise and gratitude.
And finally, we are reminded that there is a greater plan unfolding beyond what we see.

This is not meant to be read quickly.

It is meant to be returned to.

Some reflections may feel straightforward. Others may meet you in a place that is harder to define. That is part of the nature of the Psalms. They meet us where we are, but they do not leave us there.

They direct us back to God.

My hope is simple.

That these reflections would help you think clearly about what is true.
That they would steady your thinking when life feels unsettled.
And that they would remind you—again and again—that God is faithful, present, and worthy of your trust.

Not because everything is always understood.

But because He is who He is.

Introduction

This book is a quiet walk through selected portions of the Book of Psalms.

Each reflection focuses on a small passage—not to cover everything, but to consider what is most essential. The goal is not to move quickly, but to think clearly. To take what God has said and allow it to settle, one truth at a time.

The Psalms speak to every part of life. They speak when things are steady, and they speak when they are not. They give words to questions, direction in uncertainty, and reminders when we are prone to forget.

This book follows a simple path:

Knowing God.
Walking with God.
Facing difficulty.
Learning to trust.
Responding with praise.
And remembering that God's plan is greater than what we see.

Each reflection stands on its own, but together they form a steady progression—one that moves from understanding to application, from truth to response.

Take your time with it.

Return to what is helpful.

And let what is true shape how you think, how you walk, and how you rest in God.

Contents

*** KNOWING GOD ***

Before we consider how to walk with God, we must first understand who He is.

It is possible to think about God in ways that are shaped more by experience than by truth. Over time, impressions can form—some accurate, some incomplete, some simply assumed. But a steady life cannot be built on impressions. It must be built on what is true.

These Psalms begin there.

They draw our attention away from ourselves and place it where it belongs—on God. His greatness. His Word. His authority. His presence. His compassion.

We see Him as Creator, speaking the heavens into existence.

We see Him as the One whose Word restores and guides.

We see Him as sovereign, yet personal.

We see Him as patient, gracious, and fully aware of who we are.

And this is important:

We do not begin with what God asks of us.
We begin with who He is.

Because everything that follows—how we live, how we respond, how we endure—flows from that understanding.

If our view of God is unclear, our footing will be uncertain.
But when we begin to see Him rightly, something settles within us.

We are no longer trying to define life on our own.

We are learning to live in light of who He already is.

These reflections are not meant to explain everything about God. They are meant to help us see clearly what He has already revealed—so that we may walk forward with confidence, humility, and trust.

Knowing God is not the end of the journey.

But it is where the journey must begin.

When God Thinks of Us

Psalm 8:3–4

"When I consider Your heavens, the work of Your fingers,
The moon and the stars, which You have ordained;
What is man that You take thought of him,
And the son of man that You care for him?"

Reflection

There are moments when we simply need to stop and look up.

David did.

He looked at the night sky—not as a scientist measuring distance, but as a man recognizing design. The heavens were not random to him. They were the work of God's fingers. Every star placed. Every orbit sustained. Every detail held together by His will.

And in that moment, David felt something very honest:

small.

That is not a feeling we naturally pursue. We spend much of life trying to feel important, established, secure. Yet when David saw the vastness of creation, he did not feel diminished in a harmful way—he felt *rightly placed.*

Creation reminded him of two truths at once:

God is very great.

We are very small.

And yet—this is where the Psalm turns—

God thinks about us.

Not in a distant or general way. Not as one of many. But personally, attentively, intentionally.

"*What is man that You take thought of him*?"

That question is not doubt. It is wonder.

Why would the One who set the stars in place care about the details of our lives? Why would the Creator of all things give attention to people who are so limited, so often distracted, and at times so inconsistent?

And yet He does.

Scripture does not leave this as a mystery without answer. God's care is not based on our greatness, but on His nature. He is not only powerful—He is attentive. He is not only sovereign—He is personal.

To be known by God is not something we earn. It is something He chooses.

And that changes how we see ourselves.

We are not the center of creation—but we are not forgotten within it either.

There is a steadiness that comes from this truth. We do not need to prove our worth by striving for recognition, because the One who truly sees already knows us fully. At the same time, we are reminded to walk humbly, because we are part of something far greater than ourselves.

This balance—humility and value—is where a healthy life is found.

David did not walk away from the night sky discouraged.

He walked away grounded.

Supporting Scriptures

- **Genesis 1:27** — "God created man in His own image, in the image of God He created him; male and female He created them."
- **Isaiah 40:26** — "Lift up your eyes on high
And see who has created these *stars*,
The One who leads forth their host by number,
He calls them all by name;
Because of the greatness of His might and
the strength of *His* power,
Not one *of them* is missing."
- **Hebrews 2:6–7** — "What is man, that You remember him?
Or the son of man, that You are concerned about him?
7 "You have made him for a little while lower than the angels;
You have crowned him with glory and honor, And have appointed him over the works of Your hands;

Personal Application

Take time to step back from the pace of life and consider what God has made. Let creation remind you of His greatness.

Then remember this:

The same God who holds the stars also sees you.

You do not need to elevate yourself to matter. You already matter because He has chosen to care.

Walk humbly—but do not walk as if you are unseen.

Linger Thought

The One who made the heavens has not overlooked you.

The Heavens Speak

Psalm 19:1–4

"The heavens are telling of the glory of God;
And their expanse is declaring the work of His hands.
Day to day pours forth speech,
And night to night reveals knowledge.
There is no speech, nor are there words;
Their voice is not heard.
Their line has gone out through all the earth,
And their utterances to the end of the world…"

Reflection

There are messages being spoken all around us—without a single word.

David understood this. When he looked at the sky, he did not see silence. He saw testimony. The heavens were not empty space to him; they were a constant declaration of God's glory.

"*The heavens are telling…*"

Not once. Not occasionally.

Continually.

Day after day. Night after night.

This is not a message that needs translation or education. It is not limited to one nation or one people. It reaches everywhere, to everyone. The rising sun, the ordered stars, the steady rhythms of creation—all of it speaks.

And what does it say?

God is real.

God is powerful.

God has acted.

Creation does not explain everything about God, but it clearly points to Him. It is a witness that surrounds every life, whether a person pauses to consider it or not.

Yet it is possible to live under this constant testimony and still not listen.

We grow accustomed to what we see every day. The sky becomes background. The seasons become routine. The extraordinary becomes ordinary simply because it is familiar.

David did not allow that to happen.

He chose to *consider* what he saw.

That is the difference.

The message of creation is always present—but it must be noticed. And when it is, it quietly reshapes our thinking. It reminds us that life is not random, that we are not self-made, and that there is an order beyond what we control.

It also brings a certain steadiness.

If the One who established the heavens has ordered creation with such consistency, then His character is not uncertain. He is not shifting. He is not unreliable.

What He has made reflects who He is.

And while creation speaks broadly, Scripture speaks clearly. The same God who reveals Himself in the skies has made Himself known through His Word. One prepares the heart; the other gives understanding.

David saw both.

And because he saw both, he did not live as if the world was without direction.

Supporting Scriptures

- **Romans 1:20** — "For since the creation of the world His invisible attributes, His eternal power and divine nature, have been clearly seen, being understood through what has been made, so that they are without excuse."
- **Isaiah 40:26** — "Lift up your eyes on high
And see who has created these *stars*,
The One who leads forth their host by number,
He calls them all by name;
Because of the greatness of His might and
the strength of *His* power,
Not one *of them* is missing.."
- **Hebrews 11:3** — "By faith we understand that the worlds were prepared by the word of God, so

that what is seen was not made out of things which are visible.

Personal Application

Take time to notice what you normally pass by.

Look at the sky—not quickly, but thoughtfully.

Let creation remind you that God has spoken, even before you open His Word. Then return to Scripture and let that same God speak clearly and personally.

Do not let what is constant become invisible.

Linger Thought

Creation speaks of God's glory—if we will take the time to listen.

A Sure Foundation

Psalm 19:7–11

[7] The law of the Lord is perfect, restoring the soul;
The testimony of the Lord is sure, making wise the simple.
[8] The precepts of the Lord are right, rejoicing the heart;
The commandment of the Lord is pure, enlightening the eyes.
[9] The fear of the Lord is clean, enduring forever;
The judgments of the Lord are true; they are righteous altogether.
[10] They are more desirable than gold, yes, than much fine gold;
Sweeter also than honey and the drippings of the honeycomb.
[11] Moreover, by them Your servant is warned;
In keeping them there is great reward.

Reflection

After showing us how the heavens declare the glory of God, David turns to something even more direct—God's Word.

Creation speaks broadly.

But Scripture speaks clearly.

David does not describe God's Word casually. He uses words that are firm, settled, and trustworthy:

Perfect.

Sure.

Right.

Pure.

Clean.

True.

Each word builds on the next, forming a foundation that does not shift with time, culture, or opinion.

"*The law of the Lord is perfect, restoring the soul…*"

There is something deeply steady about that. The Word of God does not merely inform—it restores. It brings a person back to what is right, not by force, but by truth.

"*The testimony of the Lord is sure, making wise the simple…*"

This is not wisdom reserved for the few. It is available to those who are willing to receive it. The Word of God does not require brilliance—it requires humility.

"*The precepts of the Lord are right, rejoicing the heart…*"

Joy is not found in avoiding truth, but in aligning with it. When a person begins to walk in what is right, there is a quiet confidence that follows.

"*The commandment of the Lord is pure, enlightening the eyes…*"

God's Word does not confuse—it clarifies. It helps us see life as it truly is, not as we might wish it to be.

David is not describing something distant. He is describing something usable—something meant to guide daily life.

And then he says something that reveals his heart:

"*They are more desirable than gold…*"

This is where many of us must pause.

Do we see God's Word this way?

Not as an obligation, but as something valuable. Not as something we turn to only in difficulty, but something we return to daily because it is steady, reliable, and good.

The Word of God warns us—not to restrict us, but to protect us. It directs us—not to control us, but to guide us. It shapes us—not to diminish us, but to restore what is right.

In a world where so much changes, this remains unchanged.

And that is where a life can be anchored.

Supporting Scriptures

- **2 Timothy 3:16–17** — "[16] All Scripture is inspired by God and profitable for teaching, for reproof, for correction, for training in righteousness; [17] so that the man of God may be adequate, equipped for every good work."
- **Psalm 119:160** — "The sum of Your word is truth,
And every one of Your righteous ordinances is everlasting."
- **James 1:25** — "[25] But one who looks intently at the perfect law, the *law* of liberty, and abides by it, not having become a forgetful hearer but an effectual doer, this man will be blessed in what he does."

Personal Application

Spend time in God's Word not just to read it—but to let it shape your thinking.

Return to it when you are uncertain.
Stay in it when things are steady.

Let it restore what becomes worn, correct what drifts, and guide what lies ahead.

Do not treat it as occasional help—receive it as a sure foundation.

Linger Thought

God's Word does not shift—so a life built on it does not need to either.

When God Speaks

Psalm 33:6–9

6 By the word of the Lord the heavens were made,
And by the breath of His mouth all their host.
7 He gathers the waters of the sea together as a heap;
He lays up the deeps in storehouses.
8 Let all the earth fear the Lord;
Let all the inhabitants of the world stand in awe of Him.
9 For He spoke, and it was done;
He commanded, and it stood fast.

Reflection

There is a difference between something being made slowly—and something being made by command.

David draws our attention to that difference.

"*By the word of the Lord the heavens were made…*"

God did not struggle to create.

He did not experiment.

He did not revise.

He spoke.

And what He spoke came into being.

This is not just a statement about power—it is a statement about authority. Creation itself exists because God willed it to exist. The heavens, the earth, and all they contain are not self-originating. They are the result of His command.

"He spoke, and it was done…"

That is a kind of certainty we are not used to. In our experience, words can be uncertain. Plans can fail. Intentions can fall short. But when God speaks, there is no gap between what He says and what comes to pass.

"He commanded, and it stood fast."

What God establishes does not waver.

This matters more than we may first realize.

Because the same God who spoke creation into existence has also spoken truth into our lives. His Word is not suggestion. It is not speculation. It carries the same authority as the voice that formed the stars.

And yet, this Psalm also calls for a response:

"Let all the earth fear the Lord…"

Not fear in the sense of panic—but in the sense of rightful recognition. A settled awareness of who God is. A humility that acknowledges His authority. A reverence that shapes how we live.

We live in a time where words are often treated lightly. Promises are made and broken. Statements are adjusted. Meaning shifts.

God's Word does not follow that pattern.

When He speaks, it is true.
When He commands, it stands.

And that gives us something solid to stand on as well.

Supporting Scriptures

- **Genesis 1:3** — "[3] Then God said, "Let there be light"; and there was light."
- **Isaiah 55:11** — "So will My word be which goes forth from My mouth;
It will not return to Me empty,
Without accomplishing what I desire,
And without succeeding *in the matter* for which I sent it."
- **Hebrews 1:3** — "[3] And He is the radiance of His glory and the exact representation of His nature, and upholds all things by the word of His power. When He had made purification of sins, He sat down at the right hand of the Majesty on high,"

Personal Application

Take God's Word seriously—not out of obligation, but because of who He is.

When you read Scripture, remember:
These are not uncertain words.

They come from the One who speaks, and it is so.

Let that shape how you listen—and how you respond.

Linger Thought

When God speaks, reality responds.

Be Still

Psalm 46:10

"Cease *striving* and know that I am God;
I will be exalted among the nations, I will be exalted in the earth."

Reflection

"Cease *striving…*"

Those are not words we naturally follow.

Life moves quickly. Responsibilities press in. Thoughts race ahead. Even when we stop physically, our minds often continue moving. Stillness is not something we easily enter—it is something we must choose.

And here, it is not simply a suggestion.

It is an instruction.

"*Cease striving, and know that I am God.*"

This stillness is not about doing nothing. It is about stepping back from striving—pulling away from the constant need to manage, fix, and control everything around us.

Because much of what unsettles us comes from that very effort.

We try to hold things together that were never placed in our hands to hold.

We carry concerns as if their outcome depends entirely on us.

We rehearse possibilities, searching for certainty where none can be found.

And in doing so, we lose something important:

We lose the awareness of who God is.

"*Cease striving … and know…*"

Stillness creates space for clarity. Not new information—but remembered truth.

God is not uncertain.
God is not reacting.
God is not overwhelmed.

He is God.

That is what must be known.

The Psalm itself speaks of turmoil—nations in uproar, kingdoms shaking, the earth giving way. This is not a call to stillness because life is calm. It is a call to stillness *in the middle of disruption.*

Because stillness is not based on circumstances.

It is based on confidence in God.

To be still is to step back and recognize:

I am not in control—and I do not need to be.

God is.

And that changes how we carry what lies in front of us.

Supporting Scriptures

- **Isaiah 26:3** — "The steadfast of mind You will keep in perfect peace,
Because he trusts in You."
- **Exodus 14:14** — "The Lord will fight for you while you keep silent."
- **Mark 4:39** — "And He got up and rebuked the wind and said to the sea, "Hush, be still." And the wind died down and it became perfectly calm."

Personal Application

When your thoughts begin to race and your sense of control feels strained, pause.

Not to solve—but to remember.

Step back from what you cannot carry. Return your attention to who God is.

Stillness is not weakness. It is a quiet act of trust.

Linger Thought

Stillness is where we remember that God is already at work.

Our Dwelling Place

Psalm 90:1–2

1 Lord, You have been our dwelling place in all
generations.
2 Before the mountains were born
Or You gave birth to the earth and the world,
Even from everlasting to everlasting, You are God.

Reflection

"*Lord, You have been our dwelling place in all generations.*"

That is not how we usually think about a dwelling place.

We think of something physical—a house, a structure, a location where we feel settled and secure. Something we can see, return to, and rely on.

But here, Moses speaks of something deeper.

Not a place built by hands.

But a place found in God Himself.

"*You have been our dwelling place…*"

Not for a moment. Not for a season.

"*In all generations.*"

Before any structure existed, before any boundary was drawn, before any life began—God was already there. And He has remained.

"Before the mountains were born… from everlasting to everlasting, You are God."

Everything we know has a beginning. Everything we build has a limit. Everything we rely on in this world is, in some way, temporary.

God is not.

He does not begin.
He does not change.
He does not end.

And because of that, He is not just a place we visit—He is a place we live.

That is what Moses is expressing.

Life moves. Generations come and go. Circumstances shift. What feels stable today may not remain so tomorrow.

But God remains.

To dwell in Him is not about location—it is about dependence. It is a settled awareness that our stability does not come from what we can build or maintain, but from who He is.

That changes how we face uncertainty.

When everything around us feels temporary, we are not left without a place to stand.

We are not anchored to what fades.

We are anchored to the One who does not.

Supporting Scriptures

- **Deuteronomy 33:27** — "The eternal God is a dwelling place,
And underneath are the everlasting arms;
And He drove out the enemy from before you,
And said, 'Destroy!'"
- **John 15:4** — "Abide in Me, and I in you. As the branch cannot bear fruit of itself unless it abides in the vine, so neither *can* you unless you abide in Me.
- **Hebrews 13:8** — "Jesus Christ is the same yesterday and today and forever."

Personal Application

When life feels uncertain or unsettled, return to this truth:

Your stability is not found in what changes.

It is found in God.

Choose to rest your thoughts there.

Let your sense of security come from Him, not from what surrounds you.

Linger Thought

What is anchored in God is not shaken by time.

Compassion Without Measure

Psalm 103:8–14

8 The Lord is compassionate and gracious,
Slow to anger and abounding in lovingkindness.
9 He will not always strive *with us*,
Nor will He keep *His anger* forever.
10 He has not dealt with us according to our sins,
Nor rewarded us according to our iniquities.
11 For as high as the heavens are above the earth,
So great is His lovingkindness toward those who fear Him.
12 As far as the east is from the west,
So far has He removed our transgressions from us.
13 Just as a father has compassion on *his* children,
So the Lord has compassion on those who fear Him.
14 For He Himself knows our frame;
He is mindful that we are *but* dust.

Reflection

There are many ways people try to understand God.

Some see Him primarily as distant.
Others as demanding.
Still others as unpredictable.

But David speaks with clarity:

"The Lord is compassionate and gracious…"

These are not passing qualities. They are part of who He is.

"*Slow to anger and abounding in lovingkindness…*"

God does not respond quickly in anger. He is not short-tempered. He does not deal with us harshly at the first sign of failure. Instead, there is patience—real patience—rooted in His character.

This does not mean He overlooks sin or ignores what is wrong. But it does mean He does not deal with us as our sins deserve.

"*He has not dealt with us according to our sins…*"

That statement alone should cause us to pause.

If God were to respond to us strictly on the basis of what we deserve, none of us would stand. But His dealings with us are not based solely on justice—they are also shaped by mercy.

"*As far as the east is from the west, so far has He removed our transgressions from us.*"

That is not partial forgiveness. That is complete removal.

East and west never meet. The distance is unending. That is the picture David gives us—not to exaggerate, but to help us understand the fullness of God's forgiveness.

"*Just as a father has compassion on his children…*"

Here, David brings the truth closer.

God's compassion is not abstract. It is personal.

A good father understands the limitations of his children. He knows their weakness. He does not expect what they cannot give. He guides, corrects, and cares with understanding.

"*So the Lord has compassion on those who fear Him.*"

God knows our frame.

"*He Himself knows that we are but dust.*"

This is not a statement of worthlessness—it is a statement of understanding. God is fully aware of our limitations. He does not forget what we are made of. His compassion is not given blindly—it is given with full knowledge.

And that makes it all the more meaningful.

We are not loved because we are strong.

We are not shown mercy because we are consistent.

We are shown compassion because God is who He is.

Supporting Scriptures

- **Exodus 34:6** — "[6] Then the Lord passed by in front of him and proclaimed, "The Lord, the Lord God, compassionate and gracious, slow to anger, and abounding in lovingkindness and truth;"
- **Micah 7:18–19** — "[18] Who is a God like You,
who pardons iniquity
And passes over the rebellious act of the remnant of His possession?
He does not retain His anger forever,
Because He delights in unchanging love.
[19] He will again have compassion on us;
He will tread our iniquities under foot.
Yes, You will cast all their sins
Into the depths of the sea."
- **Hebrews 4:15–16** — "[15] For we do not have a high priest who cannot sympathize with our weaknesses, but One who has been tempted in all things as *we are, yet* without sin. [16] Therefore let us draw near with confidence to the throne of grace, so that we may receive mercy and find grace to help in time of need.

Personal Application

When you are aware of your own shortcomings, do not pull away from God.

Come to Him.

Remember that His response is not based on impatience, but on compassion. Walk in reverence, but do not approach Him as if He is unwilling to receive you.

Let His mercy shape how you see both Him—and yourself.

Linger Thought

God's compassion is not limited by our weakness—it is revealed in it.

Fully Known

Psalm 139:1–6

139 O Lord, You have searched me and known *me*.
2 You know when I sit down and when I rise up;
You understand my thought from afar.
3 You scrutinize my path and my lying down,
And are intimately acquainted with all my ways.
4 Even before there is a word on my tongue,
Behold, O Lord, You know it all.
5 You have enclosed me behind and before,
And laid Your hand upon me.
6 *Such* knowledge is too wonderful for me;
It is *too* high, I cannot attain to it.

Reflection

There is a difference between being seen—and being known.

Most of us are seen by many people throughout life. But to be known—truly known—is something far deeper. It means nothing is hidden. Nothing is misunderstood. Nothing is overlooked.

David says something remarkable:

"*O Lord, You have searched me and known me.*"

Not partially. Not generally.

Completely.

"*You know when I sit down and when I rise up…*"

God is aware of the ordinary moments—the movements that make up a day. Nothing is too small to escape His notice.

"*You understand my thought from afar.*"

Even what has not yet been spoken is known to Him. Thoughts that are still forming, concerns that have not been expressed—God understands them fully.

"*You scrutinize my path and my lying down…*"

Every direction. Every step. Every pause.

"*And are intimately acquainted with all my ways.*"

There is nothing about our lives that is unfamiliar to Him.

That can feel unsettling at first.

To be fully known means that nothing is hidden—not our thoughts, not our motives, not our failures. We cannot present a version of ourselves to God that is more polished than reality.

But David does not respond with fear or withdrawal.

He responds with awe.

"*Such knowledge is too wonderful for me…*"

Why?

Because being fully known by God is not paired with rejection.

It is paired with presence.

God's knowledge of us is not cold observation—it is relational awareness. He knows us as we are, yet

He does not turn away. He understands fully, yet He remains near.

There is a kind of rest found in that.

We no longer need to maintain appearances before God. We no longer need to explain ourselves in order to be understood. We are already known—completely.

And that allows us to come to Him honestly.

Not carefully managing what we reveal.
Not holding back what we would rather hide.

But bringing our lives as they are.

Because nothing we bring will surprise Him.

Supporting Scriptures

- **Jeremiah 17:10** — "I, the Lord, search the heart, I test the mind, Even to give to each man according to his ways, According to the results of his deeds."
- **Hebrews 4:13** — "[13] And there is no creature hidden from His sight, but all things are open and laid bare to the eyes of Him with whom we have to do."
- **John 2:24–25** — "[24] But Jesus, on His part, was not entrusting Himself to them, for He knew all men, [25] and because He did not need anyone to testify concerning man, for He Himself knew what was in man."

Personal Application

Come to God honestly.

There is no need to hide what He already sees or to explain what He already understands. Speak openly with Him—about your thoughts, your concerns, and even your struggles.

Let His complete knowledge of you become a reason for trust, not distance.

Linger Thought

You are fully known—and still welcomed.

Search Me

Psalm 139:23–24

23 Search me, O God, and know my heart;
Try me and know my anxious thoughts;
24 And see if there be any hurtful way in me,
And lead me in the everlasting way.

Reflection

It is one thing to be known by God.

It is another thing to invite Him to search us.

David does both.

"*Search me, O God, and know my heart…*"

This is not a casual request. It is a deliberate opening of the inner life—thoughts, motives, desires—everything that is often hidden even from ourselves.

We tend to examine outward actions. God examines the heart.

"*Try me and know my anxious thoughts…*"

David is not asking God to look only at what is settled and strong. He is inviting Him into what is unsettled—into worry, fear, and uncertainty.

This is an honest prayer.

Because much of what shapes our lives is not visible to others. It lives beneath the surface. And if left unexamined, it quietly directs our thinking and decisions.

"*See if there be any hurtful way in me…*"

That requires humility.

To ask this is to acknowledge that we may not see ourselves clearly. That there may be patterns, attitudes, or responses that are not right, even if they feel natural to us.

David is not defending himself.

He is asking to be shown.

"*And lead me in the everlasting way.*"

This is the purpose of the request.

Not simply to be examined—but to be guided.

God's searching is not meant to expose and leave us there. It is meant to reveal and then lead. To bring what is hidden into the light, and then direct us toward what is lasting and true.

There is a kind of safety in this prayer.

Because it places our inner life in the hands of One who sees clearly and leads rightly.

We do not have to rely on our own ability to fully understand ourselves. We can ask God to do what we cannot do completely on our own.

And then we can follow where He leads.

Supporting Scriptures

- **Psalm 26:2** — "Examine me, O Lord, and try me; Test my mind and my heart."
- **Proverbs 20:27** — "The spirit of man is the lamp of the Lord, Searching all the innermost parts of his being."
- **2 Corinthians 13:5** — "[5] Test yourselves *to see* if you are in the faith; examine yourselves! Or do you not recognize this about yourselves, that Jesus Christ is in you—unless indeed you fail the test?"

Personal Application

Take time to ask God to search your heart.

Not quickly, and not defensively—but honestly.

Be willing to see what He reveals.

And be willing to follow where He leads.

Growth begins when we allow truth to reach beneath the surface.

Linger Thought

When we invite God to search us, we open the way for Him to lead us.

A Gracious King

Psalm 145:8–13

[8] The Lord is gracious and merciful;
Slow to anger and great in lovingkindness.
[9] The Lord is good to all,
And His mercies are over all His works.
[10] All Your works shall give thanks to You, O Lord,
And Your godly ones shall bless You.
[11] They shall speak of the glory of Your kingdom
And talk of Your power;
[12] To make known to the sons of men Your mighty acts
And the glory of the majesty of Your kingdom.
[13] Your kingdom is an everlasting kingdom,
And Your dominion *endures* throughout all generations.

Reflection

When we think of a king, we often think of authority, power, and rule.

And rightly so.

But David gives us a fuller picture of God's kingship—one that is not only strong, but deeply good.

"*The Lord is gracious and merciful…*"

This is where David begins.

Not with power alone, but with character.

God's authority is not harsh. It is not cold. It is not distant. His rule is shaped by grace and mercy. He does not use His power to oppress, but to sustain, to guide, and to care.

"*Slow to anger and great in lovingkindness…*"

His patience is not short-lived. His kindness is not limited. These are not occasional expressions—they are consistent qualities of who He is.

"*The Lord is good to all, and His mercies are over all His works.*"

God's goodness is not narrow. It extends broadly across what He has made. His care is not selective or unpredictable—it is steady and far-reaching.

"*All Your works shall give thanks to You…*"

Creation itself reflects His goodness. And those who know Him respond with praise—not because they are compelled, but because they recognize who He is.

"*They shall speak of the glory of Your kingdom…*"

God's kingdom is not hidden. It is not uncertain. It is something that can be spoken of with confidence, because it is real and enduring.

"*Your kingdom is an everlasting kingdom…*"

Every earthly authority fades. Every system built by man eventually weakens or changes.

God's kingdom does not.

It is not temporary.

It is not fragile.

It does not depend on circumstances.

It endures.

And so does His rule.

"The Lord sustains all who fall and raises up all who are bowed down."

This is where His kingship becomes personal.

God is not only ruling over all—He is attentive to individuals. He sees those who struggle. He upholds those who are weak. He does not overlook those who are bowed down under the weight of life.

A king with that kind of authority—and that kind of compassion—is not one to fear in distance, but one to trust closely.

Supporting Scriptures

- **Exodus 34:6** — "[6] Then the Lord passed by in front of him and proclaimed, "The Lord, the Lord God, compassionate and gracious, slow to anger, and abounding in lovingkindness and truth;"
- **Daniel 4:34** — "[34] But at the end of that period, I, Nebuchadnezzar, raised my eyes toward heaven and my reason returned to me, and I blessed the Most High and praised and honored Him who lives forever; For His dominion is an everlasting dominion,
And His kingdom *endures* from generation to generation."
- **Matthew 11:28–30** — "[28]Come to Me, all who are weary and heavy-laden, and I will give you rest. [29] Take My yoke upon you and learn from Me, for I am gentle and humble in heart, and you will find

rest for your souls. [30] For My yoke is easy and My burden is light."

Personal Application

Remember that God's authority is not separate from His goodness.

When you think of His rule, do not think only of power—think also of grace.

Trust Him not just because He is able, but because He is good.

Linger Thought

God rules with power—but also with compassion.

*** WALKING WITH GOD ***

Knowing who God is where life begins.

But it is not where it remains.

There is a difference between understanding truth and living in it. One informs the mind. The other shapes the path. What we have seen about God must now begin to guide how we walk each day.

These Psalms move us from foundation to practice.

They show us that a life with God is not formed in moments of inspiration, but in patterns of direction. In what we return to. In what we choose. In how we respond when no one else is watching.

We see the importance of guarding what influences us.

We are reminded to seek God's ways rather than rely on our own.

We learn that humility opens the door to guidance.

We are called to trust, to commit, and to walk steadily—even when the path is not fully clear.

This is not a call to perfection.

It is a call to consistency.

Walking with God is not about moving quickly—it is about moving rightly. Step by step. Choice by choice. Over time, a life begins to reflect where it has been walking.

And this is where growth takes place.

Not all at once.

But steadily.

As we continue forward, these reflections are meant to help us consider not just what we believe—but how we live.

Because a life that walks with God will, over time, begin to look like it.

Rooted and Steady

Psalm 1:1–3

1 How blessed is the man who does not walk in
the counsel of the wicked,
Nor stand in the path of sinners,
Nor sit in the seat of scoffers!
2 But his delight is in the law of the Lord,
And in His law he meditates day and night.
3 He will be like a tree *firmly* planted by streams of water,
Which yields its fruit in its season
And its leaf does not wither;
And in whatever he does, he prospers.

Reflection

Every life is shaped by something.

Not always in obvious ways. Not always in a single moment. But steadily, over time, what we allow into our thinking begins to influence how we live.

Psalm 1 begins with a contrast.

"*Blessed is the man who does not walk… stand… sit…*"

There is a progression here.

Walking suggests exposure—being around certain influences.

Standing suggests acceptance—lingering where we once passed by.

Sitting suggests settling—becoming comfortable in what once may have been resisted.

What begins subtly can become established.

And so the Psalm begins with a caution—not to withdraw from life, but to be mindful of what shapes us.

Then it turns:

"*But his delight is in the law of the Lord…*"

This is the difference.

Not simply avoiding what is harmful, but choosing what is right.

"*On His law he meditates day and night.*"

This is not occasional attention. It is steady return. A pattern of thinking shaped over time by God's Word.

And the result is a picture that is both simple and strong:

"*He will be like a tree firmly planted by streams of water…*"

Not a tree struggling to survive—but one that is rooted.

The source of strength is not in the tree itself, but in where it is planted.

"*Which yields its fruit in its season…*"

Growth is not forced. It comes at the right time.

"*And its leaf does not wither…*"

There is stability, even when conditions change.

"*And in whatever he does, he prospers.*"

This is not a promise of ease or success by the world's definition. It is a picture of a life that is steady, fruitful, and aligned with what is right.

A life that is not easily shaken.

This Psalm does not present a complicated path.

It presents a clear one.

Be careful what shapes you.

Delight in what is true.

Return to it often.

And over time, your life will reflect where you are rooted.

Supporting Scriptures

- **Joshua 1:8** — "[8] This book of the law shall not depart from your mouth, but you shall meditate on it day and night, so that you may be careful to do according to all that is written in it; for then you will make your way prosperous, and then you will have success."
- **Jeremiah 17:7–8** — "[7]Blessed is the man who trusts in the Lord
And whose trust is the Lord.
[8] "For he will be like a tree planted by the water,
That extends its roots by a stream
And will not fear when the heat comes;
But its leaves will be green,
And it will not be anxious in a year of drought
Nor cease to yield fruit"

- **Colossians 2:6–7** — "[6] Therefore as you have
received Christ Jesus the Lord, *so* walk in
Him, [7] having been firmly rooted *and now* being built
up in Him and established in your faith, just as
you were instructed, *and* overflowing with gratitude."

Personal Application

Pay attention to what is shaping your thinking.

Choose to spend time in God's Word—not occasionally, but consistently. Let it guide your thoughts and influence your decisions.

Over time, this quiet pattern will lead to a life that is steady and fruitful.

Linger Thought

What you return to daily is what you will be rooted in.

Who May Dwell

Psalm 15:1–5

1 O Lord, who may abide in Your tent?
Who may dwell on Your holy hill?
2 He who walks with integrity, and works righteousness,
And speaks truth in his heart.
3 He does not slander with his tongue,
Nor does evil to his neighbor,
Nor takes up a reproach against his friend;
4 In whose eyes a reprobate is despised,
But who honors those who fear the Lord;
He swears to his own hurt and does not change;
5 He does not put out his money at interest,
Nor does he take a bribe against the innocent.
He who does these things will never be shaken.

Reflection

There is a question at the beginning of this Psalm that is both simple and searching:

"*O Lord, who may abide in Your tent?*
Who may dwell on Your holy hill?"

It is not a question about location.
It is a question about relationship.

Who lives in a way that reflects closeness with God?

David does not answer with feelings or intentions.
He answers with character.

"He who walks with integrity..."

Not perfection—but consistency. A life that is not divided between what is shown and what is hidden.

"And works righteousness..."

Not occasional right actions, but a pattern of living aligned with what is true.

"And speaks truth in his heart."

Not only outward honesty, but inward truthfulness. A refusal to shape reality to fit preference. A willingness to see clearly, even when it is uncomfortable.

"He does not slander with his tongue..."

Words matter. They can build or damage. A life that walks with God is careful not to use words to diminish others.

"Nor does evil to his neighbor..."

This reaches beyond speech into action. It is a call to live in a way that does not harm, exploit, or disregard others.

"He honors those who fear the Lord..."

There is a recognition here of what is truly valuable. Respect is not given based on status, but on reverence for God.

"He swears to his own hurt and does not change..."

This is a life of reliability. Commitments are kept, even when they become difficult. Integrity does not shift with convenience.

"*He does not put out his money at interest, nor take a bribe…*"

There is fairness here. A refusal to take advantage of others for personal gain.

And then the Psalm closes with a steady promise:

"*He who does these things will never be shaken.*"

Not because life will be easy—but because the foundation is right.

This Psalm does not describe how a person earns a relationship with God. It describes what a life shaped by Him begins to look like.

These qualities are not produced by effort alone. They are formed over time as a person walks with God and aligns with His truth.

It is a picture—not of perfection—but of direction.

Supporting Scriptures

- **Micah 6:8** — "He has told you, O man, what is good;
And what does the Lord require of you
But to do justice, to love kindness,
And to walk humbly with your God?"
- **James 1:22** — "But prove yourselves doers of the word, and not merely hearers who delude themselves."
- **1 Peter 1:15–16** — "but like the Holy One who called you, be holy yourselves also in all *your* behavior; [16] because it is written, "You shall be holy, for I am holy."

Personal Application

Consider your daily life—not just what you believe, but how you live.

Are your words truthful?
Are your actions consistent?
Are your commitments reliable?

Walking with God is not only seen in what we say—it is revealed in how we live.

Linger Thought

A life close to God is shaped by truth, integrity, and consistency.

Clean Hands, Pure Heart

Psalm 24:3–5
3 Who may ascend into the hill of the Lord?
And who may stand in His holy place?
4 He who has clean hands and a pure heart,
Who has not lifted up his soul to falsehood
And has not sworn deceitfully.
5 He shall receive a blessing from the Lord
And righteousness from the God of his salvation.

Reflection

"*Who may ascend into the hill of the Lord?*
And who may stand in His holy place?"

It is a question of access.

Not access to a location—but access to the presence of God.

David answers clearly:

"*He who has clean hands and a pure heart…*"

Clean hands speak of outward life—what we do, how we act, the visible patterns of our behavior.

A pure heart speaks of inward life—what we desire, what we think, what we hold onto beneath the surface.

God does not separate the two.

It is possible to appear right outwardly while holding onto what is not right inwardly. It is also possible to desire what is right but fail to follow through in action. But a life that walks closely with God brings both together.

Clean hands.

Pure heart.

"*Who has not lifted up his soul to falsehood...*"

This points to where our trust is placed.

To lift up the soul to something false is to give weight, attention, or dependence to what is not true. It is to rely on something that cannot ultimately hold.

A life aligned with God does not build itself on what is unstable.

"*And has not sworn deceitfully...*"

There is honesty here—both in word and intention. A refusal to manipulate truth for personal advantage.

Then comes the result:

"*He shall receive a blessing from the Lord and righteousness from the God of his salvation.*"

This is not a transaction—it is a response.

A life that aligns with God's ways is a life that experiences His favor—not as something earned, but as something that flows from walking rightly.

This Psalm does not call for perfection.

It calls for alignment.

A life that is being shaped—both outwardly and inwardly—by what is true.

Supporting Scriptures

- **Matthew 5:8** — "Blessed are the pure in heart, for they shall see God."
- **James 4:8** — "Draw near to God and He will draw near to you. Cleanse your hands, you sinners; and purify your hearts, you double-minded"
- **1 Samuel 16:7** — "But the Lord said to Samuel, "Do not look at his appearance or at the height of his stature, because I have rejected him; for God *sees* not as man sees, for man looks at the outward appearance, but the Lord looks at the heart."

Personal Application

Pay attention to both your actions and your inner life.

Do not settle for outward correctness alone. Allow God to shape what is beneath the surface as well.

Seek to live with integrity that is both seen and unseen.

Linger Thought

God looks beyond what we do—He sees who we are becoming.

Teach Me Your Ways

Psalm 25:4–5

4 Make me know Your ways, O Lord;
Teach me Your paths.
5 Lead me in Your truth and teach me,
For You are the God of my salvation;
For You I wait all the day.

Reflection

There is a posture in these words that is easy to overlook—but essential to a life that walks with God.

"*Make me know Your ways, O Lord;*
Teach me Your paths."

David is not assuming he already understands.

He is asking to be taught.

That alone sets the tone.

Much of life is shaped by what we think we already know. We form opinions, develop patterns, and move forward based on our own understanding. But David steps back from that and takes a different approach:

He asks God to lead.

"*Lead me in Your truth and teach me…*"

This is not a request for information alone—it is a request for direction.

To be taught by God means more than learning facts. It means allowing His truth to shape how we think, how we decide, and how we live.

"*For You are the God of my salvation…*"

This is why David trusts Him.

God is not a distant instructor. He is personally involved. He is the One who rescues, sustains, and leads. His guidance is not detached—it is rooted in relationship.

"*For You I wait all the day.*"

There is patience here.

Learning God's ways is not immediate. It is not always quick or clear in the moment. It requires waiting—being willing to pause, to listen, and to follow in His timing rather than forcing our own.

This kind of waiting is not passive.

It is attentive.

It is the willingness to say:

I do not have to figure everything out on my own.

I am willing to be led.

That posture keeps a person teachable.

And a teachable heart is one that continues to grow.

Supporting Scriptures

- **Proverbs 3:5–6** — "[5] Trust in the Lord with all your heart
And do not lean on your own understanding.
[6] In all your ways acknowledge Him,
And He will make your paths straight."
- **Isaiah 30:21** — "Your ears will hear a word behind you, "This is the way, walk in it," whenever you turn to the right or to the left."
- **James 1:5** — "But if any of you lacks wisdom, let him ask of God, who gives to all generously and without reproach, and it will be given to him."

Personal Application

Approach each day with a willingness to be taught.

Do not rely only on what you already understand. Ask God to guide your thinking and direct your steps.

Be patient as you wait for His direction, and be ready to follow when it becomes clear.

Linger Thought

A teachable heart is a guided life.

He Leads the Humble

Psalm 25:8–10

8 Good and upright is the Lord;
Therefore He instructs sinners in the way.
9 He leads the humble in justice,
And He teaches the humble His way.
10 All the paths of the Lord are lovingkindness and truth
To those who keep His covenant and His testimonies.

Reflection

"*Good and upright is the Lord…*"

David begins with who God is.

Before speaking about guidance, direction, or instruction, he anchors everything in God's character. God is not uncertain. He is not inconsistent. He is good—and He is upright.

Because of that:

"*He instructs sinners in the way.*"

This is a gracious truth.

God does not wait for people to become worthy before He begins to guide them. He instructs those who need direction—those who recognize they do not already know the way.

"*He leads the humble in justice,*
And He teaches the humble His way."

Humility is central here.

Not weakness.

Not self-doubt.

But a clear recognition:

I do not see everything clearly.

I need guidance.

A humble person is teachable. Not resistant. Not defensive. Willing to be corrected, willing to be redirected.

And it is that posture that God responds to.

He leads the humble.

Not those who insist on their own way.

Not those who are unwilling to reconsider.

But those who are open to being shaped.

"*All the paths of the Lord are lovingkindness and truth…*"

God's ways are not divided.

They are not sometimes kind and sometimes true.

They are both.

His guidance will never lead outside of truth, and it will never be separate from His goodness. Even when His direction is difficult, it is still right—and it is still grounded in His care.

"*To those who keep His covenant and His testimonies.*"

There is a response required.

God's guidance is not given for observation alone—it is given to be followed. To walk in His ways means to receive what He has said and to live accordingly.

This Psalm reminds us that God is not reluctant to guide.

But the path begins with humility.

Supporting Scriptures

- **Proverbs 11:2** — "When pride comes, then comes dishonor, But with the humble is wisdom."
- **Isaiah 66:2** — "For My hand made all these things, Thus all these things came into being," declares the Lord. "But to this one I will look, To him who is humble and contrite of spirit, and who trembles at My word."
- **James 4:6** — "But He gives a greater grace. Therefore *it* says, "God is opposed to the proud, but gives grace to the humble."

Personal Application

Approach God with humility.

Be willing to admit when you do not understand. Be open to correction and direction.

As you do, trust that His guidance will always be both true and good.

Linger Thought

God leads those who are willing to be led.

Trust and Commit

Psalm 37:3–5

[3] Trust in the Lord and do good;
Dwell in the land and cultivate faithfulness.
[4] Delight yourself in the Lord;
And He will give you the desires of your heart.
[5] Commit your way to the Lord,
Trust also in Him, and He will do it.

Reflection

There are times in life when direction feels unclear and outcomes feel uncertain.

In those moments, we often look for something specific to do—something that will bring clarity or control. David gives us a simple, steady pattern:

"*Trust in the Lord and do good…*"

Trust comes first.

Not because action is unimportant, but because action without trust can become anxious and driven. Trust settles the heart before it directs the hands.

To trust in the Lord is to place confidence in who He is—His character, His wisdom, His ability to lead. It is not a vague feeling. It is a deliberate reliance.

"*And do good…*"

Trust does not lead to inactivity. It leads to right action. We continue to live faithfully in what is in front of us, even when we do not see the full path ahead.

"*Dwell in the land and cultivate faithfulness.*"

There is a steadiness here.

Stay where God has placed you.

Be consistent in what is right.

Do not drift or become unsettled simply because outcomes are not immediate.

"*Delight yourself in the Lord…*"

This moves deeper.

Not just trusting Him for what He provides—but finding satisfaction in who He is. When delight shifts from circumstances to God Himself, the heart becomes less dependent on changing conditions.

"*And He will give you the desires of your heart.*"

This is often misunderstood.

As we delight in God, our desires begin to align with His. What we long for becomes shaped by what is right and lasting. And in that alignment, we begin to experience what He has intended for us.

"*Commit your way to the Lord…*"

To commit is to place something fully into another's care.

This is not partial.

It is not conditional.

It is the willingness to entrust our direction, our plans, and our outcomes to Him.

"*Trust also in Him, and He will do it.*"

God is not passive.

When we trust Him and commit our way to Him, He is at work—often in ways we do not immediately see, but always in ways that are consistent with His truth and His purpose.

This Psalm does not remove uncertainty.

It gives us a way to walk through it.

Supporting Scriptures

- **Proverbs 3:5–6** — "Trust in the Lord with all your heart And do not lean on your own understanding. [6] In all your ways acknowledge Him, And He will make your paths straight."
- **Matthew 6:33** — "But seek first His kingdom and His righteousness, and all these things will be added to you."
- **Romans 8:28** — "And we know that God causes all things to work together for good to those who love God, to those who are called according to *His* purpose."

Personal Application

Place your trust in God before you act.

Continue doing what is right, even when results are not immediate. Learn to find your satisfaction in Him, not in outcomes.

Commit your path to Him—and trust that He is at work.

Linger Thought

When your way is committed to God, your steps are no longer uncertain.

Established Steps

Psalm 37:23–24

23 The steps of a man are established by the Lord,
And He delights in his way.
24 When he falls, he will not be hurled headlong,
Because the Lord is the One who holds his hand.

Reflection

"*The steps of a man are established by the Lord…*"

That is a steady truth.

Life often feels uncertain because we do not see the full path ahead. We think in terms of outcomes, long-term direction, and how everything will unfold. But this Psalm speaks in smaller terms:

Steps.

Not the entire journey at once—just the next step.

And those steps, David says, are established by the Lord.

This does not mean that every moment is easy or clearly understood. It means that God is actively involved in the direction of a life that is aligned with Him.

"*And He delights in his way.*"

God is not distant from the path we walk. He is attentive to it. He takes interest in it. There is a personal element here—He is not merely guiding from afar, but engaged in the details.

"*When he falls, he will not be hurled headlong…*"

This is an important part of the picture.

The path is not described as flawless.

There will be missteps. There will be moments where we stumble, where our footing is not steady. But the promise is not that we will never fall—it is that we will not be abandoned in it.

"*Because the Lord is the One who holds his hand.*"

This is where the steadiness comes from.

Not from our ability to walk perfectly.
But from God's willingness to hold on.

A child learning to walk does not succeed because of perfect balance, but because of support. The hand that steadies them makes the difference.

So it is with us.

Our security is not found in flawless movement through life, but in God's faithful involvement in each step.

He establishes.
He sustains.
He holds.

And because of that, even when we stumble, we are not lost.

Supporting Scriptures

- **Proverbs 16:9** — "The mind of man plans his way, but the Lord directs his steps."
- **Isaiah 41:13** — "For I am the Lord your God, who upholds your right hand,
Who says to you, 'Do not fear, I will help you.'"
- **Jude 1:24** — " Now to Him who is able to keep you from stumbling, and to make you stand in the presence of His glory blameless with great joy,"

Personal Application

Focus on the step in front of you.

You do not need to see the entire path to move forward faithfully. Walk in what you know is right, and trust God with what lies ahead.

When you stumble, do not assume you have been left behind.

God is still holding your hand.

Linger Thought

Your steps are steady—not because you never fall, but because God holds you when you do.

Guarding the Heart

Psalm 119:9–11

9 How can a young man keep his way pure?
By keeping *it* according to Your word.
10 With all my heart I have sought You;
Do not let me wander from Your commandments.
11 Your word I have treasured in my heart,
That I may not sin against You.

Reflection

"*How can a young man keep his way pure?*"

It is a direct question.

Not theoretical.

Not abstract.

It is about real life—about how a person lives in a way that is right in the midst of influence, pressure, and distraction.

The answer is just as direct:

"*By keeping it according to Your word.*"

Purity of life does not come from good intentions alone. It is shaped by alignment with what God has said. His Word becomes the standard—not opinion, not culture, not preference.

"*With all my heart I have sought You…*"

There is intentionality here.

This is not casual interest. It is a deliberate pursuit. A choosing to seek God—not occasionally, but with the whole heart.

"*Do not let me wander from Your commandments.*"

David recognizes something important:

We are capable of drifting.

Not all at once.

Not dramatically.

But gradually.

Without attention, without return to truth, we begin to move off course.

That is why this prayer matters.

"*Your word I have treasured in my heart…*"

This is more than reading.

It is storing. Holding. Keeping close.

God's Word is not meant to remain external—it is meant to become internal. To shape thoughts, guide decisions, and influence responses before actions are taken.

"*That I may not sin against You.*"

This reveals the purpose.

God's Word is not given simply to inform—it is given to guard. It helps us recognize what is right before we move in the wrong direction. It strengthens us to respond differently when faced with choice.

The heart is where life is directed.

What is held there will eventually be lived out.

And so David makes a choice:

He fills his heart with what is true—so that his life will follow.

Supporting Scriptures

- **Proverbs 4:23** — "Watch over your heart with all diligence, For from it *flow* the springs of life."
- **Colossians 3:16** — " Let the word of Christ richly dwell within you, with all wisdom teaching and admonishing one another with psalms *and* hymns *and* spiritual songs, singing with thankfulness in your hearts to God."
- **Matthew 4:4** — "But He answered and said, "It is written, 'Man shall not live on bread alone, but on every word that proceeds out of the mouth of God.""

Personal Application

Be intentional about what you place in your heart.

Spend time in God's Word not just to read it, but to retain it. Let it shape your thinking and guide your responses.

Guard your heart by filling it with what is true.

Linger Thought

What you store in your heart will shape the path you walk.

A Light for the Path

Psalm 119:105

Your word is a lamp to my feet
And a light to my path.

Reflection

"*Your word is a lamp to my feet
And a light to my path.*"

There is something important in the way this is said.

Not a floodlight.
Not a full view of everything ahead.

A lamp.

Just enough light for the next step.

We often want more than that.

We want to see the entire path—where it leads, how it unfolds, what lies ahead. We look for certainty before we move. But God's Word is described differently.

It gives light—but in measure.

It shows what we need to see now, not everything we wish to know about later.

A lamp to my feet.

That is close. Immediate. Personal. It helps us see where we are placing our next step. It keeps us from stumbling over what is right in front of us.

A light to my path.

That is direction. Not full clarity, but enough to know which way to go.

This requires trust.

Because it means walking forward without seeing the entire journey. It means relying on God's Word daily—not once, not occasionally, but consistently.

Light that is not used does not guide.

And light that is ignored does not help.

God's Word is given so that we do not walk in darkness—so that our decisions, our direction, and our responses are shaped by what is true rather than what is uncertain.

It does not remove the need for faith.

It supports it.

Step by step, it provides what is needed.

Not all at once.

But always enough.

Supporting Scriptures

- **Proverbs 6:23** — "For the commandment is a lamp and the teaching is light;
And reproofs for discipline are the way of life"
- **2 Peter 1:19** — "*So* we have the prophetic word *made* more sure, to which you do well to pay

attention as to a lamp shining in a dark place, until the day dawns and the morning star arises in your hearts."

- **John 8:12** — "Then Jesus again spoke to them, saying, "I am the Light of the world; he who follows Me will not walk in the darkness, but will have the Light of life."

Personal Application

Do not wait for full clarity before you move forward.

Return to God's Word and take the next step it makes clear. Trust Him for what you cannot yet see.

Walk in the light you have been given.

Linger Thought

God's Word does not show everything ahead—but it always shows the next step.

A Blessed Life

Psalm 128:1–2

1 How blessed is everyone who fears the Lord,
Who walks in His ways.
2 When you shall eat of the fruit of your hands,
You will be happy and it will be well with you.

Reflection

"*How blessed is everyone who fears the Lord,
Who walks in His ways.*"

This Psalm begins with a statement that is both simple and clear.

A blessed life is not defined by circumstance. It is defined by direction.

To "*fear the Lord*" is not to live in anxiety, but in reverence. It is a settled recognition of who God is—His authority, His holiness, His rightful place in our lives.

And that reverence is not meant to remain inward.

It is expressed in how we live.

"*Who walks in His ways.*"

This is where belief becomes visible.

Walking in God's ways means aligning daily life with what He has said. It is not occasional obedience, but a steady pattern. Not perfection—but direction.

It is choosing what is right even when it is not convenient.

It is remaining faithful even when no one else sees.

"*When you shall eat of the fruit of your hands…*"

There is a sense of provision here. Not excess, not indulgence—but the satisfaction of what is rightly gained.

"*You will be happy and it will be well with you.*"

This is not a promise of an easy life.

It is a promise of a *rightly ordered life.*

There is a difference.

Happiness in this sense is not based on changing conditions. It is rooted in alignment with God. When life is lived in His ways, there is a steadiness beneath the surface—even when circumstances are not ideal.

"*It will be well with you.*"

That is a quiet statement.

Not dramatic.

Not exaggerated.

But deeply reassuring.

A life that walks with God is not without difficulty—but it is not without stability.

There is a kind of peace that comes from knowing you are walking where you should be.

Supporting Scriptures

- **Deuteronomy 10:12** — "Now, Israel, what does the Lord your God require from you, but to fear the Lord your God, to walk in all His ways and love Him, and to serve the Lord your God with all your heart and with all your soul,"
- **Ecclesiastes 12:13** — "The conclusion, when all has been heard, *is*: fear God and keep His commandments, because this *applies to* every person."
- **John 14:21** — "He who has My commandments and keeps them is the one who loves Me; and he who loves Me will be loved by My Father, and I will love him and will disclose Myself to him."

Personal Application

Consider the direction of your daily life.

Are you walking in God's ways—not just in intention, but in practice?

Let reverence for God shape your choices, and trust that a life aligned with Him will be steady, even when it is not easy.

Linger Thought

A blessed life is not found in ease—but in walking rightly with God.

*** WHEN LIFE IS HARD ***

There are seasons in life that do not unfold as we expect.

Questions remain unanswered.
Circumstances linger longer than we hoped.
And at times, what we feel does not match what we know to be true.

These are not unusual moments.

They are part of life.

The Psalms do not avoid these seasons. They speak directly into them. Not with shallow answers, and not with forced conclusions—but with honesty.

We hear questions that are not quickly resolved.
We see burdens that feel heavy and ongoing.
We recognize emotions that are real—fear, confusion, discouragement, even silence.

And yet, through all of it, one thing remains consistent:

The direction is still toward God.

These Psalms show us that difficulty is not a place where faith disappears. It is often where faith becomes most evident.

Not because everything is clear.

But because we continue to turn to Him anyway.

We are reminded that we can speak honestly with God. That we can bring what is unsettled without needing to first make it sound resolved. That we can ask, wait, struggle, and still remain anchored.

Life may not always feel steady.

But God is.

And in these moments, that is what we return to.

Not quick answers.

Not easy explanations.

But a steady God—who remains present, even when the path is hard.

How Long, O Lord?

Psalm 13:1–2

1 How long, O Lord? Will You forget me forever?
How long will You hide Your face from me?
2 How long shall I take counsel in my soul,
Having sorrow in my heart all the day?
How long will my enemy be exalted over me?

Reflection

There are moments in life when time feels heavy.

Not because of how much has happened—but because of how long something has remained unresolved.

David puts words to that experience:

"*How long, O Lord?*"

It is not a question of information.
It is a question of endurance.

"*How long will You forget me? Forever?*"

This is not a statement of fact—it is an expression of feeling. David knows God has not truly forgotten him. But in the waiting, in the silence, it *feels* that way.

And he says it.

This is an important part of the Psalm.

David does not hide what he is experiencing. He does not soften his words to make them sound more composed. He speaks honestly, even when his thoughts are unsettled.

"*How long will You hide Your face from me?*"

There are times when God's presence does not feel near. Not because He has moved, but because our awareness of Him is clouded by difficulty, delay, or uncertainty.

"*How long shall I take counsel in my soul… having sorrow in my heart all the day?*"

Left to ourselves, we begin to turn things over repeatedly in our own thinking. We try to reason through what we cannot resolve. And in doing so, sorrow deepens—not always because circumstances worsen, but because we carry them alone.

"*How long will my enemy be exalted over me?*"

Whether the pressure comes from people, circumstances, or internal struggle, the sense of being overcome can feel real and ongoing.

And still, David speaks.

This is what the Psalm teaches us:

There is a place for honest questions before God.

Not questions that accuse—but questions that express.

Not questions that reject—but questions that reach.

David does not turn away in frustration.

He turns toward God in honesty.

And that is where this kind of prayer belongs.

Supporting Scriptures

- **Psalm 10:1** — "Why do You stand afar off, O Lord? Why do You hide *Yourself* in times of trouble?"
- **Habakkuk 1:2** — "How long, O Lord, will I call for help, And You will not hear?
I cry out to You, "Violence!"
Yet You do not save."
- **2 Corinthians 1:8** — "For we do not want you to be unaware, brethren, of our affliction which came *to us* in Asia, that we were burdened excessively, beyond our strength, so that we despaired even of life;"

Personal Application

When waiting feels long and clarity does not come, speak honestly with God.

Do not withdraw or remain silent. Bring your questions to Him—not to challenge His character, but to express your need.

Let honesty draw you closer, not push you away.

Linger Thought

God is not distant from your questions—He invites you to bring them to Him.

Yet I Will Trust

Psalm 13:5–6

5 But I have trusted in Your lovingkindness;
My heart shall rejoice in Your salvation.
6 I will sing to the Lord,
Because He has dealt bountifully with me.

Reflection

Psalm 13 begins with a question:

"*How long, O Lord?*"

It ends with a decision.

"*But I have trusted in Your lovingkindness…*"

Nothing in the Psalm suggests that David's circumstances have changed. There is no indication that the waiting has ended or that the difficulty has been removed.

What has changed is his focus.

"*But I have trusted…*"

This is not a feeling.

It is a choice.

Trust, in this moment, is not based on what David sees. It is based on what he knows to be true about God. Specifically:

"*Your lovingkindness.*"

God's faithful, consistent, covenant love.

Not temporary.
Not uncertain.
Not dependent on circumstances.

David turns from his questions to God's character.

"*My heart shall rejoice in Your salvation.*"

Notice the progression.

He does not say, *my situation will change.*
He says, *my heart shall rejoice.*

This is an inward shift.

Joy, in this case, is not tied to resolution—it is tied to confidence. Confidence that God is still at work, still present, and still faithful.

"*I will sing to the Lord…*"

Even here—before the answer comes—David chooses to respond with praise.

Not because everything is clear.
But because God is.

"*Because He has dealt bountifully with me.*"

This is not denial of present difficulty.

It is remembrance.

David looks back and recalls what God has already done. Past faithfulness becomes the foundation for present trust.

This is how the Psalm moves:

From question…
To trust…

To joy…
To praise.

And all of it happens before the circumstances change.

Supporting Scriptures

- **Lamentations 3:21–23** — "[21] This I recall to my mind, Therefore I have hope.
[22] The Lord's lovingkindnesses indeed never cease,
For His compassions never fail.
[23] *They* are new every morning;
Great is Your faithfulness."
- **Romans 15:13** — "Now may the God of hope fill you with all joy and peace in believing, so that you will abound in hope by the power of the Holy Spirit."
- **Hebrews 13:8** — "Jesus Christ is the same yesterday and today and forever."

Personal Application

When answers do not come quickly, choose where you will place your focus.

Return to what you know is true about God.
Remember His past faithfulness.
Let that shape your present response.

Trust is often a decision made before anything changes.

Linger Thought

Trust begins when we choose to rest in who God is, not in what we see.

Near in the Breaking

Psalm 34:18

The Lord is near to the brokenhearted
And saves those who are crushed in spirit.

Reflection

"*The Lord is near to the brokenhearted…*"

There are times when life does not feel strong or steady.

It feels broken.

Not just difficult—but inwardly fractured. Expectations unmet. Loss experienced. Things not turning out as hoped. And in those moments, the question is not always spoken, but often felt:

Where is God in this?

David answers directly.

"*The Lord is near…*"

Not distant.
Not removed.
Not observing from afar.

Near.

This does not mean that the pain disappears. It does not mean that everything is immediately restored. But it does mean that the brokenhearted are not alone in what they are experiencing.

God does not wait for strength before He draws close.

He draws near in the breaking.

"*And saves those who are crushed in spirit.*"

There is a depth here.

To be "*crushed in spirit*" is to feel pressed down—to the point where strength seems diminished and direction unclear. It is not outward weakness alone, but inward weight.

And this is where God acts.

He saves.

Not always by removing the situation immediately, but by sustaining, restoring, and bringing a person through what feels overwhelming.

God's nearness is not reserved for moments of clarity and strength.

It is often most evident in moments of weakness.

This runs against how we sometimes think.

We may assume that we must gather ourselves, become steady, and regain control before coming to God. But this Psalm shows the opposite.

Brokenness does not push God away.

It draws Him near.

Supporting Scriptures

- **Isaiah 57:15** — "For thus says the high and exalted One
Who lives forever, whose name is Holy,
"I dwell *on* a high and holy place,
And *also* with the contrite and lowly of spirit
In order to revive the spirit of the lowly
And to revive the heart of the contrite."
- **Matthew 5:4** — "Blessed are those who mourn, for they shall be comforted."
- **2 Corinthians 12:9** — "And He has said to me, "My grace is sufficient for you, for power is perfected in weakness." Most gladly, therefore, I will rather boast about my weaknesses, so that the power of Christ may dwell in me."

Personal Application

When your heart feels heavy or broken, do not assume that God is distant.

Come to Him as you are.

You do not need to wait until you feel strong. His nearness is often most clearly experienced in the moments when you are not.

Linger Thought

God draws near—not after the breaking, but within it.

Speak to Your Soul

Psalm 42:5

Why are you in despair, O my soul?
And *why* have you become disturbed within me?
Hope in God, for I shall again praise Him
For the help of His presence.

Reflection

"*Why are you in despair, O my soul?*
And why have you become disturbed within me?"

This is an unusual moment.

The psalmist is not speaking to others. He is speaking to himself.

There are times when emotions rise without invitation. Discouragement settles in. Thoughts turn inward. And before long, the weight begins to shape how everything is seen.

The psalmist does not ignore this.

He acknowledges it.

"*Why are you in despair…?*"

This is not denial. It is recognition.

But he does not stop there.

"*Hope in God…*"

He directs his soul.

This is important.

Feelings are real, but they are not meant to lead. If left unexamined, they can begin to define reality in ways that are not accurate or helpful. The psalmist chooses instead to speak truth into what he is feeling.

Hope is not found in the situation changing immediately.

It is placed in God.

"*For I shall again praise Him…*"

There is confidence here—not in the present moment, but in what will come. The psalmist looks forward, not because everything is resolved, but because he knows God is still at work.

"*The help of my countenance and my God.*"

God is not distant from this struggle. He is described as help—personal, present, and sufficient.

This Psalm shows us something we all need to learn:

We must not only listen to our thoughts—we must also speak to them.

Left alone, discouragement can deepen. But when truth is brought in—clearly, intentionally—it begins to change the direction of the heart.

Not instantly.

But steadily.

Supporting Scriptures

- **Lamentations 3:24** — "The Lord is
my portion," says my soul,
"Therefore I have hope in Him."
- **Psalm 103:1** — "Bless the Lord, O my soul,
And all that is within me, *bless* His holy name."
- **2 Corinthians 10:5** — "*We are* destroying speculations and every lofty thing raised up against the knowledge of God, and *we are* taking every thought captive to the obedience of Christ,"

Personal Application

When discouragement begins to take hold, pause and examine what you are thinking.

Do not allow your thoughts to move unchecked. Bring truth into them. Remind yourself of who God is and where your hope is found.

Speak truth, even when your feelings have not yet caught up.

Linger Thought

Do not let your thoughts lead alone—guide them with truth.

When Understanding Fails

Psalm 44:23–26

23 Arouse Yourself, why do You sleep, O Lord?
Awake, do not reject us forever.
24 Why do You hide Your face
And forget our affliction and our oppression?
25 For our soul has sunk down into the dust;
Our body cleaves to the earth.
26 Rise up, be our help,
And redeem us for the sake of Your lovingkindness.

Reflection

There are times when life does not make sense.

Not just difficult—but confusing.

The psalmist describes a situation where suffering has come, yet there is no clear reason for it. There has been no turning away from God, no obvious cause that explains the hardship. And in that place, the words come:

"*Awake, why do You sleep, O Lord?*"

This is not a statement about God's nature. It is a cry from experience.

From the psalmist's perspective, God seems inactive. Silent. Unresponsive.

"*Why do You hide Your face…?*"

The sense of distance is real.

This is one of the hardest places to stand—not knowing why something is happening, and not seeing any immediate answer from God.

"*For our soul has sunk down into the dust…*"

There is weight here. Not just physical difficulty, but inward heaviness. The kind that settles into the heart and affects everything.

"*Rise up, be our help…*"

The psalmist calls out—not with polished words, but with urgency.

And then he anchors his request:

"*And redeem us for the sake of Your lovingkindness.*"

Even here, in confusion, the appeal is made to God's character.

Not to personal merit.
Not to understanding.
But to His faithful love.

This is what stands out in this Psalm.

The psalmist does not have clarity—but he still turns to God.

He does not have answers—but he still calls out.

He does not resolve the situation—but he refuses to walk away from the One who can.

This kind of prayer does not come from certainty.

It comes from dependence.

Supporting Scriptures

- **Isaiah 55:8–9** — "[8] For My thoughts are
not your thoughts,
Nor are your ways My ways," declares the Lord.
[9] "For *as* the heavens are higher than the earth,
So are My ways higher than your ways
And My thoughts than your thoughts."
- **Job 13:15** — "Though He slay me,
I will hope in Him.
Nevertheless I will argue my ways before Him."
- **Romans 8:26** — " In the same way the Spirit also helps our weakness; for we do not know how to pray as we should, but the Spirit Himself intercedes for *us* with groanings too deep for words;"

Personal Application

When you do not understand what God is doing, do not withdraw.

Bring your confusion to Him. Speak honestly. Ask for help.

Even without answers, you can still anchor yourself in His character.

Linger Thought

When understanding fails, trust can still remain.

Overwhelmed Within

Psalm 55:4–8

4 My heart is in anguish within me,
And the terrors of death have fallen upon me.
5 Fear and trembling come upon me,
And horror has overwhelmed me.
6 I said, "Oh, that I had wings like a dove!
I would fly away and be at rest.
7 "Behold, I would wander far away,
I would lodge in the wilderness. *Selah.*
8 "I would hasten to my place of refuge
From the stormy wind *and* tempest."

Reflection

"*My heart is in anguish within me…*"

There are moments when pressure does not stay on the outside.

It moves inward.

What begins as a situation becomes a weight that settles in the heart. Thoughts begin to circle. Emotions rise. And what was once manageable begins to feel overwhelming.

David does not hide that.

"*Terrors of death have fallen upon me.*
Fear and trembling come upon me…"

This is not mild concern.

This is deep distress.

David describes both physical and emotional response—fear, trembling, a sense of being overtaken. It is the kind of experience that disrupts normal thinking and makes everything feel unstable.

"*Horror has overwhelmed me.*"

There is no attempt here to minimize what he is feeling.

And then he says something many have felt, even if they have not said it out loud:

"*Oh, that I had wings like a dove!*
I would fly away and be at rest."

This is the desire to escape.

Not to solve the situation—but to leave it.

To get away from the pressure, the noise, the weight. To find a place where the strain is no longer present.

"*I would wander far away…*
I would lodge in the wilderness…"

Distance feels like relief.

Silence feels like safety.

"*I would hasten to my place of refuge*
From the stormy wind and tempest."

The imagery is clear.

Life feels like a storm—and the natural response is to look for a way out.

This Psalm reminds us of something important:

Even those who walk closely with God can feel overwhelmed.

David is not distant from God when he says these things. He is bringing these thoughts directly to Him.

He does not pretend strength.

He expresses reality.

And that is where this kind of honesty belongs.

Supporting Scriptures

- **2 Corinthians 1:8** — "For we do not want you to be unaware, brethren, of our affliction which came *to us* in Asia, that we were burdened excessively, beyond our strength, so that we despaired even of life;"
- **Psalm 61:2** — "From the end of the earth I call to You when my heart is faint;
Lead me to the rock that is higher than I."
- **Matthew 11:28** — "Come to Me, all who are weary and heavy-laden, and I will give you rest."

Personal Application

When you feel overwhelmed, do not hide it or ignore it.

Bring it to God.

You do not need to pretend strength. You do not need to have everything settled before you come to Him.

Let your honesty be the starting point.

Linger Thought

God does not turn away from your weakness—He meets you in it.

Cast Your Burden

Psalm 55:22

Cast your burden upon the Lord and He will sustain you; He will never allow the righteous to be shaken.

Reflection

"*Cast your burden upon the Lord…*"

There is a difference between carrying something—and casting it.

To carry is to hold onto it, to keep it close, to manage its weight as best we can. And often, that is what we do. We carry concerns, responsibilities, and uncertainties as if they must remain in our hands.

But this verse calls for something more deliberate.

Cast.

To cast is to release. To place what we are holding into someone else's care.

Not partially.

Not temporarily.

Fully.

"*Your burden…*"

This is personal.

Not a general idea of stress or pressure—but the specific weight you are carrying. The concerns that stay with you. The thoughts that return. The things you are trying to manage on your own.

God does not ask us to ignore them.

He invites us to bring them.

"*Upon the Lord…*"

This is where the burden is placed.

Not into uncertainty.

Not into distraction.

But into the care of God Himself.

"*And He will sustain you.*"

This is the promise.

Not necessarily that the burden disappears immediately—but that you will not be left to carry it alone. God provides what is needed to remain steady under what would otherwise overwhelm.

"*He will never allow the righteous to be shaken.*"

This is not a guarantee of an easy path.

It is a guarantee of stability.

A life that is anchored in God may face difficulty, but it is not ultimately undone by it.

Casting our burden is not a one-time action.

It is a repeated choice.

Because what we release today has a way of returning tomorrow. And when it does, we are invited again to place it back where it belongs.

Supporting Scriptures

- **1 Peter 5:7** — "casting all your anxiety on Him, because He cares for you."
- **Philippians 4:6–7** — "[6] Be anxious for nothing, but in everything by prayer and supplication with thanksgiving let your requests be made known to God. [7] And the peace of God, which surpasses all comprehension, will guard your hearts and your minds in Christ Jesus."
- **Psalm 68:19** — "Blessed be the Lord, who daily bears our burden,
The God *who* is our salvation. "

Personal Application

Identify what you are carrying today.

Do not hold onto it as if it depends entirely on you. Bring it to God—specifically and intentionally—and release it into His care.

When it returns to your thoughts, return it again.

Linger Thought

What you release to God no longer has to be carried alone.

When the Heart Turns Bitter

Psalm 73:21–26

21 When my heart was embittered
And I was pierced within,
22 Then I was senseless and ignorant;
I was *like* a beast before You.
23 Nevertheless I am continually with You;
You have taken hold of my right hand.
24 With Your counsel You will guide me,
And afterward receive me to glory.
25 Whom have I in heaven *but You*?
And besides You, I desire nothing on earth.
26 My flesh and my heart may fail,
But God is the strength of my heart and my portion
forever.

Reflection

"*When my heart was embittered…*"

This is a quiet admission—but an important one.

Bitterness does not always arrive suddenly. It often grows slowly, beneath the surface. It begins with disappointment, confusion, or comparison, and over time it hardens into something deeper.

David describes it plainly.

"*I was pierced within.*"

There is an inward effect. Bitterness does not stay contained—it begins to shape how we see, how we think, and how we respond.

"*Then I was senseless and ignorant…*"

This is a moment of clarity.

Looking back, David recognizes that his thinking had become distorted. Not because he lacked intelligence—but because his perspective had shifted away from truth.

"*I was like a beast before You.*"

That is a strong statement.

It describes a life reacting rather than understanding. Driven by feeling rather than guided by truth.

And then the Psalm turns.

"*Nevertheless I am continually with You…*"

Despite his confusion.

Despite his bitterness.

God had not left him.

"*You have taken hold of my right hand.*"

Even when David's thinking was off course, God's hold remained steady.

"*With Your counsel You will guide me…*"

God's guidance is not withdrawn because of our struggle. He continues to lead, to correct, and to restore perspective.

"*And afterward receive me to glory.*"

There is a long view here.

Life is not limited to what is immediately seen. God's purposes extend beyond present circumstances.

*"Whom have I in heaven but You?
And besides You, I desire nothing on earth."*

This is a reordering of the heart.

What once seemed pressing is now placed in its proper position.

"My flesh and my heart may fail…"

There is honesty again.

Weakness is real.
Limitations are real.

"But God is the strength of my heart and my portion forever."

This is where David settles.

Not in his understanding.
Not in his circumstances.

But in God.

Bitterness lost its hold—not because everything changed outwardly, but because something changed inwardly.

Truth returned.
Perspective was restored.

Supporting Scriptures

- **Hebrews 12:15** — "See to it that no one comes short of the grace of God; that no root of bitterness springing up causes trouble, and by it many be defiled;"
- **Proverbs 3:5** — "Trust in the Lord with all your heart And do not lean on your own understanding."
- **Lamentations 3:22–23** —

"22 The Lord's lovingkindnesses indeed never cease,
For His compassions never fail.
23 *They* are new every morning;
Great is Your faithfulness."

Personal Application

Pay attention to what is forming beneath the surface of your heart.

If bitterness begins to take hold, do not ignore it. Bring it before God. Allow Him to restore your perspective and re-center your thinking on what is true.

Return your focus to Him.

Linger Thought

When the heart turns back to God, bitterness begins to lose its hold.

Remember in the Dark

Psalm 77:7–12

7 Will the Lord reject forever?
And will He never be favorable again?
8 Has His lovingkindness ceased forever?
Has *His* promise come to an end forever?
9 Has God forgotten to be gracious,
Or has He in anger withdrawn His compassion? *Selah.*
10 Then I said, "It is my grief,
That the right hand of the Most High has changed."
11 I shall remember the deeds of the Lord;
Surely I will remember Your wonders of old.
12 I will meditate on all Your work
And muse on Your deeds.

Reflection

There are times when questions come quickly—and answers do not.

"*Will the Lord reject forever?*
And will He never be favorable again?"

These are not casual thoughts.

They rise in seasons where clarity is absent and circumstances feel heavy. The psalmist is not pretending strength. He is expressing what the moment feels like.

"Has His lovingkindness ceased forever?
Has His promise come to an end forever?"

These questions press deeper.

When difficulty continues, it can begin to affect how we think about God. Not because His character has changed—but because our perspective has been clouded by what we are experiencing.

"Has God forgotten to be gracious…?"

This is where the struggle reaches its edge.

And then something shifts.

"Then I said, 'It is my grief,
That the right hand of the Most High has changed.'"

The psalmist recognizes that the problem is not with God.

It is with his perception.

In the middle of distress, it had begun to feel as though God had changed. But God had not changed—his understanding had.

And so he makes a deliberate decision:

"I shall remember the deeds of the Lord…"

This is the turning point.

When present circumstances feel uncertain, he looks back. Not to escape the present, but to anchor himself in what is known to be true.

"I will remember Your wonders of old.
I will meditate on all Your work
And muse on Your deeds."

This is not a passing thought.

It is intentional remembrance.

He brings to mind what God has already done—His faithfulness, His power, His consistent care. And as he does, his thinking begins to realign.

The darkness does not immediately disappear.

But it no longer defines everything.

Because truth has been brought back into view.

Supporting Scriptures

- **Lamentations 3:21** — "This I recall to my mind, therefore I have hope…"
- **Malachi 3:6** — "For I, the Lord, do not change; therefore you, O sons of Jacob, are not consumed."
- **Deuteronomy 7:9** — "Know therefore that the Lord your God, He is God, the faithful God, who keeps His covenant and His lovingkindness to a thousandth generation with those who love Him and keep His commandments;"

Personal Application

When your thoughts begin to question God's character, pause.

Do not let the moment define what is true. Instead, intentionally remember what God has already done.

Let past faithfulness steady your present thinking.

Linger Thought

When the present feels uncertain, remember what has always been true.

Still Calling Out

Psalm 88:1–3

1 O Lord, the God of my salvation,
I have cried out by day and in the night before You.
2 Let my prayer come before You;
Incline Your ear to my cry!
3 For my soul has had enough troubles,
And my life has drawn near to Sheol.

Reflection

There are Psalms that rise into hope.

This one does not—at least not in the way we might expect.

"*O Lord, the God of my salvation…*"

Even here, at the beginning, there is something steady.

God is still addressed. Still recognized. Still named as the One who saves.

But what follows is heavy.

"*I have cried out by day and in the night before You.*"

This is not a passing prayer.

It is ongoing. Repeated. Persistent.

"*Let my prayer come before You;*
Incline Your ear to my cry!"

There is urgency.

A desire to be heard. A need for God's attention—not because He is unaware, but because the weight of the moment is pressing in.

"For my soul has had enough troubles…"

There is no softening of words here.

The psalmist does not try to reframe the situation in a positive way. He does not quickly move to resolution. He speaks plainly.

Life feels overwhelming.

"My life has drawn near to Sheol."

This is the depth of the struggle.

A sense of being near the end. Not necessarily physically, but emotionally and spiritually exhausted.

And yet—

He is still speaking to God.

That is what stands out.

This Psalm does not resolve in the same way others do. It does not move quickly into praise or clear hope. But it does something just as important:

It continues.

It continues to address God.
It continues to cry out.
It continues to bring what is real into His presence.

This is a kind of faith that is often overlooked.

Not the faith that sees clearly.
But the faith that continues—even when it does not.

There are seasons where clarity comes quickly.

And there are seasons where it does not.

In those moments, faith may look like this:

Still calling out.

Still turning toward God.

Still bringing what is heavy, even when no answer has yet come.

And that, too, matters.

Supporting Scriptures

- **Lamentations 3:8** — "Even when I cry out and call for help,
He shuts out my prayer."
- **Romans 8:26** — "In the same way the Spirit also helps our weakness; for we do not know how to pray as we should, but the Spirit Himself intercedes for *us* with groanings too deep for words;"
- **2 Corinthians 4:8–9** — " *we are* afflicted in every way, but not crushed; perplexed, but not despairing; [9] persecuted, but not forsaken; struck down, but not destroyed;"

Personal Application

When you do not feel relief and answers seem delayed, do not stop turning to God.

Continue to bring your thoughts, your concerns, and your struggles to Him.

Faith is not only seen in clarity—it is also seen in persistence.

Linger Thought

Even when answers are delayed, calling out to God is never wasted.

*** TRUSTING GOD ***

There is a difference between knowing what is true and resting in it.

Trust is where that difference is settled.

Up to this point, we have seen who God is, and we have considered what it means to walk in His ways. But there are moments when understanding and effort are not enough—when the path is unclear, when the outcome is uncertain, and when control is out of reach.

This is where trust becomes essential.

Not as a feeling—but as a decision.

These Psalms lead us into that place.

They show us how to set our focus on God, not on what surrounds us.

They remind us that His presence is steady, even when life is not.

They call us to wait, to rest, and to remain anchored when we cannot see what lies ahead.

Trust does not require full visibility.

It requires confidence in who God is.

We are not asked to understand everything.

We are asked to rely on Him.

And as we do, something begins to change—not always the situation, but the way we stand within it.

Trust steadies the heart.

It quiets what would otherwise overwhelm.

It allows us to move forward—not because we have control, but because we know the One who does.

This is not a passive life.

It is a settled one.

A life that rests, not in certainty of outcomes, but in certainty of God.

Set Before Me

Psalm 16:8–9

8 I have set the Lord continually before me;
Because He is at my right hand, I will not be shaken.
9 Therefore my heart is glad and my glory rejoices;
My flesh also will dwell securely.

Reflection

"I have set the Lord continually before me…"

This is a deliberate choice.

David does not say that God is occasionally in his thoughts, or that he remembers Him only in moments of need. He says that he has *set* the Lord before him—intentionally, consistently.

This is not about God moving closer.

It is about David choosing where to place his attention.

In a world filled with shifting concerns, distractions, and uncertainties, what we keep in front of us matters. It shapes how we think, how we respond, and how we interpret what is happening around us.

David chooses to keep God in view.

"Because He is at my right hand, I will not be shaken."

The right hand is a place of support and strength.

God is not distant from David's life. He is present, near, and actively sustaining. And because of that, David speaks with confidence:

"I will not be shaken."

Not because difficulty is absent.

But because stability is present.

"Therefore my heart is glad and my glory rejoices…"

Joy follows this perspective.

Not a surface-level happiness, but a settled gladness rooted in confidence. When God is kept before us, the heart is no longer driven by uncertainty—it is steadied by truth.

"My flesh also will dwell securely."

There is a sense of rest here.

Not because everything is controlled, but because everything is entrusted.

David's security is not based on predicting outcomes or managing circumstances.

It is based on proximity to God.

And that proximity is not accidental—it is chosen.

"I have set the Lord continually before me."

This is where trust begins.

Supporting Scriptures

- **Isaiah 26:3** — "The steadfast of mind You will keep in perfect peace,
Because he trusts in You."
- **Hebrews 12:2** — "fixing our eyes on Jesus, the author and perfecter of faith, who for the joy set before Him endured the cross, despising the shame, and has sat down at the right hand of the throne of God."
- **Colossians 3:2** — "Set your mind on the things above, not on the things that are on earth."

Personal Application

Be intentional about what you keep before you.

Return your thoughts to God regularly throughout the day. Let His presence shape your perspective.

As you do, you will find that your stability does not depend on circumstances, but on where your focus remains.

Linger Thought

Where you place your focus will shape how steady you stand.

The Shepherd's Care

Psalm 23

1 The Lord is my shepherd,
I shall not want.
2 He makes me lie down in green pastures;
He leads me beside quiet waters.
3 He restores my soul;
He guides me in the paths of righteousness
For His name's sake.
4 Even though I walk through the valley of the shadow of
death,
I fear no evil, for You are with me;
Your rod and Your staff, they comfort me.
5 You prepare a table before me in the presence of my
enemies;
You have anointed my head with oil;
My cup overflows.
6 Surely goodness and lovingkindness will follow me all the
days of my life,
And I will dwell in the house of the Lord forever.

Reflection

"*The Lord is my shepherd…*"

That is where David begins.

Not with a situation.

Not with a need.

But with a relationship.

A shepherd is not distant from the sheep. He is present, attentive, and responsible for their care. The sheep do not guide themselves—they are led.

"*The Lord is my shepherd…*"

This is personal.

Not *a* shepherd.

My shepherd.

"*I shall not want.*"

This does not mean that every desire is fulfilled. It means that what is truly needed will not be lacking. The Shepherd provides what is necessary, even when the path is not fully understood.

"*He makes me lie down in green pastures…*"

There is rest here.

Not rest that is forced, but rest that is provided. A place of provision and calm—given, not achieved.

"*He leads me beside quiet waters…*"

The Shepherd does not drive. He leads.

There is direction, but also care in how that direction is given.

"*He restores my soul…*"

There are times when strength fades. When energy is low. When the inner life feels worn.

The Shepherd restores.

"*He guides me in the paths of righteousness*
For His name's sake."

The path is not random. It is purposeful.

God leads in ways that are right—not only for our good, but because it reflects who He is.

"Even though I walk through the valley of the shadow of death…"

The path is not without difficulty.

There are valleys. There are dark places. There are moments where the way forward feels uncertain.

"I fear no evil…"

Not because the valley is safe.

"But because You are with me."

This is the difference.

The presence of the Shepherd changes the experience of the valley.

"Your rod and Your staff, they comfort me."

The tools of the Shepherd—guidance and protection—bring reassurance, not fear.

"You prepare a table before me…"

Even in the presence of difficulty, there is provision.

"You have anointed my head with oil;
My cup overflows."

There is care. There is abundance—not necessarily in circumstance, but in how God meets the need.

"Surely goodness and lovingkindness will follow me all the days of my life…"

This is not uncertainty.

It is confidence.

"And I will dwell in the house of the Lord forever."

The journey has a destination.

Not temporary.
Not uncertain.
But lasting.

Supporting Scriptures

- **John 10:11** — "I am the good shepherd; the good shepherd lays down His life for the sheep."
- **Isaiah 40:11** — "Like a shepherd He will tend His flock,
In His arm He will gather the lambs
And carry *them* in His bosom;
He will gently lead the nursing *ewes*."
- **Hebrews 13:20–21** — "[20] Now the God of peace, who brought up from the dead the great Shepherd of the sheep through the blood of the eternal covenant, *even* Jesus our Lord, [21] equip you in every good thing to do His will, working in us that which is pleasing in His sight, through Jesus Christ, to whom *be* the glory forever and ever. Amen."

Personal Application

Remember that you are not guiding your life alone.

God is not distant—He is leading.

Trust His direction, even when the path is not fully clear. Rest in His care, especially when life feels uncertain.

Linger Thought

The Shepherd's presence is what makes the path secure.

The Lord Is My Light

Psalm 27:1

The Lord is my light and my salvation;
Whom shall I fear?
The Lord is the defense of my life;
Whom shall I dread?

Reflection

"*The Lord is my light and my salvation;*
Whom shall I fear?
The Lord is the defense of my life;
Whom shall I dread?"

David does not begin with his circumstances.

He begins with God.

"*The Lord is my light…*"

Light reveals what is true. It removes uncertainty. It allows us to see clearly what is around us and where we are going. Without light, everything becomes unclear—shadows grow, and even small things can appear overwhelming.

To say that the Lord is our light is to say that clarity is found in Him. Not in our own understanding, not in changing circumstances—but in who He is and what He reveals.

"*...and my salvation...*"

God is not only the One who shows the way—He is the One who delivers. Salvation is not something we produce. It is something He provides.

"*...the defense of my life...*"

This speaks of protection.

Not the absence of difficulty, but the presence of security. God Himself is described as the stronghold—the place where life is guarded and held.

And because of these truths, David asks:

"*Whom shall I fear? ... Whom shall I dread?*"

These are not questions looking for answers.

They are statements of confidence.

Fear often grows when we focus on what is uncertain, what is threatening, or what is beyond our control. But David directs his attention elsewhere—toward God.

When God is seen clearly, fear begins to lose its hold.

Not because the situation disappears, but because it is no longer the highest thing in view.

God is.

This does not remove every feeling of concern. It does not mean that life will never feel heavy or uncertain. But it does provide something stronger than fear:

A steady confidence in who God is.

And that changes how we stand.

Supporting Scriptures

- **Isaiah 12:2** — "Behold, God is my salvation,

I will trust and not be afraid;
For the Lord God is my strength and song,
And He has become my salvation."

- **John 8:12** — "hen Jesus again spoke to them, saying, "I am the Light of the world; he who follows Me will not walk in the darkness, but will have the Light of life."
- **Romans 8:31** — "What then shall we say to these things? If God *is* for us, who *is* against us?"

Personal Application

When fear begins to rise, shift your focus.

Do not ignore what is happening—but do not let it become your primary view. Return your attention to who God is—your light, your salvation, your defense.

Let that truth steady your thinking.

Linger Thought

When God is your light, fear no longer leads the way.

Wait with Courage

Psalm 27:13–14

13 *I would have despaired* unless I had believed that I would
see the goodness of the Lord
In the land of the living.
14 Wait for the Lord;
Be strong and let your heart take courage;
Yes, wait for the Lord.

Reflection

"*I would have despaired unless I had believed…*"

David speaks plainly.

Without belief—without a settled confidence in God—despair would have taken hold. Not gradually, but fully.

This is an important admission.

Faith is not an added comfort.
It is what keeps the heart from giving way.

"*That I would see the goodness of the Lord*
In the land of the living."

David is not speaking about a distant future alone. He is looking for God's goodness to be evident in the present—in real life, in real time.

Not always immediately.

Not always clearly.

But truly.

And because of that, he gives this instruction:

"*Wait for the Lord.*"

Waiting is one of the most difficult parts of walking with God.

Not because it is passive—but because it requires trust without immediate confirmation. It means holding steady when outcomes are not yet visible.

"*Be strong and let your heart take courage…*"

Strength, in this context, is not force.

It is steadiness.

Courage is not the absence of difficulty.

It is the willingness to remain when the situation is not yet resolved.

"*Yes, wait for the Lord.*"

David repeats it.

Because waiting is not something we do once.

It is something we return to.

Again and again.

This is not a call to inactivity.

It is a call to remain anchored—to hold to what is true about God, even when the timing of His work is not yet clear.

David does not deny the difficulty of waiting.

But he shows us how to stand within it.

Supporting Scriptures

- **Isaiah 40:31** — "Yet those who wait for the Lord
Will gain new strength;
They will mount up *with* wings like eagles,
They will run and not get tired,
They will walk and not become weary."
- **Lamentations 3:25–26** — "25 The Lord is good to those who wait for Him,
To the person who seeks Him.
26 *It is* good that he waits silently
For the salvation of the Lord."
- **Romans 8:25** — "But if we hope for what we do not see, with perseverance we wait eagerly for it."

Personal Application

When you are waiting, do not assume that nothing is happening.

Remain steady. Hold to what you know is true about God. Let your heart take courage—not from immediate results, but from His character.

Waiting is not wasted when it is anchored in Him.

Linger Thought

Waiting with God is not empty—it is where strength is formed.

Our Refuge

Psalm 46:1–3

1 God is our refuge and strength,
A very present help in trouble.
2 Therefore we will not fear, though the earth should change
And though the mountains slip into the heart of the sea;
3 Though its waters roar *and* foam,
Though the mountains quake at its swelling pride. *Selah.*

Reflection

"*God is our refuge and strength…*"

David does not begin with the situation.

He begins with God.

A refuge is a place of safety—a place to go when what is outside is unstable. It is not where life always happens, but where we return when life feels uncertain or threatened.

God is described as that place.

Not partially.

Not occasionally.

But fully.

"*And a very present help in trouble.*"

Not distant help.

Not delayed help.

Present.

In the moment of trouble—not after it has passed. God is not removed from difficulty. He is near within it.

"*Therefore we will not fear…*"

This is the response.

Not because trouble is absent.

But because God is present.

"*Though the earth should change…*"

Even when what feels stable begins to shift.

"*And though the mountains slip into the heart of the sea…*"

Even when what seems immovable begins to move.

"*Though its waters roar and foam…*"

Even when circumstances become chaotic.

"*Though the mountains quake at its swelling pride…*"

Even when everything feels unsettled.

These are not small disturbances.

They describe upheaval—situations where normal expectations no longer hold.

And still:

"*We will not fear.*"

Not because the situation is controlled.

But because God is.

This Psalm does not promise that life will remain calm.

It reminds us where to go when it is not.

God is not simply someone who helps us endure difficulty.

He is the place we return to within it.

Supporting Scriptures

- **Psalm 62:6–7** — "[6] He only is my rock and my salvation,
My stronghold; I shall not be shaken.
[7] On God my salvation and my glory *rest*;
The rock of my strength, my refuge is in God."
- **Isaiah 41:10** — "'Do not fear, for I am with you; Do not anxiously look about you, for I am your God. I will strengthen you, surely I will help you, Surely I will uphold you with My righteous right hand.'"
- **Hebrews 13:6** — "so that we confidently say,
"The Lord is my helper, I will not be afraid.
What will man do to me?""

Personal Application

When life feels unstable, do not try to hold everything together on your own.

Return to God as your refuge.

Let His presence steady you, even when circumstances remain unsettled.

Linger Thought

When everything around you shifts, God remains the place you can stand.

When I Am Afraid

Psalm 56:3–4

3 When I am afraid,
I will put my trust in You.
4 In God, whose word I praise,
In God I have put my trust;
I shall not be afraid.
What can *mere* man do to me?

Reflection

"*When I am afraid…*"

David does not say *if*.

He says *when*.

Fear is not presented as something that never happens. It is acknowledged as part of life. There are moments when uncertainty rises, when circumstances press in, and when the mind begins to consider what could go wrong.

David does not deny that.

He names it.

But he does not stop there.

"*When I am afraid,*
I will put my trust in You."

This is a decision made in the moment of fear.

Not after it passes.

Not once everything feels calm again.

Right there—in the middle of it.

Fear may come, but it does not have to remain in control.

"*In God, whose word I praise…*"

David anchors his trust in something specific:

God's Word.

Not his own reasoning.

Not his own ability to manage the situation.

God has spoken—and that is what David returns to.

"*In God I have put my trust;*
I shall not be afraid."

This is not a contradiction.

David has already said that fear comes. But here he is describing its place—it does not lead. It does not define his response.

Trust has taken that place.

"*What can mere man do to me?*"

Fear often grows when we focus on what others may do, what might happen, or what is beyond our control. But David shifts his perspective.

He measures the situation in light of God.

And when he does, fear begins to lose its weight.

This Psalm does not teach us how to avoid fear.

It shows us what to do when it comes.

Supporting Scriptures

- **Isaiah 12:2** — "Behold, God is my salvation,

I will trust and not be afraid;
For the Lord God is my strength and song,
And He has become my salvation."

- **2 Timothy 1:7** — "For God has not given us

a spirit of timidity, but of power and love
and discipline."

- **Hebrews 13:6** — "so that we confidently say,

"The Lord is my helper, I will not be afraid.
What will man do to me?"

Personal Application

When fear rises, do not wait for it to pass before responding.

Choose, in that moment, to place your trust in God. Return to what He has said. Let His truth guide your thinking instead of your fear.

Linger Thought

Fear may come—but it does not have to lead.

Quiet Rest

Psalm 62:5–8

5 My soul, wait in silence for God only,
For my hope is from Him.
6 He only is my rock and my salvation,
My stronghold; I shall not be shaken.
7 On God my salvation and my glory *rest*;
The rock of my strength, my refuge is in God.
8 Trust in Him at all times, O people;
Pour out your heart before Him;
God is a refuge for us. *Selah.*

Reflection

"*My soul, wait in silence for God only…*"

David is speaking to himself again.

Not because he lacks understanding—but because he knows how easily the heart becomes unsettled. Thoughts begin to move, concerns begin to rise, and before long, the inner life becomes noisy.

So he gives direction:

Wait.

In silence.

For God alone.

This is not empty silence.

It is a quieting of the soul—pulling attention away from everything competing for it and placing it fully on God.

"For my hope is from Him."

Hope is not drawn from circumstances. It is not built on outcomes.

It is rooted in God.

"He only is my rock and my salvation…"

David narrows his focus.

Not many sources. Not divided trust.

God alone.

"My stronghold; I shall not be shaken."

There is stability here.

Not because life is steady—but because God is.

"On God my salvation and my glory rest…"

What matters most—security, identity, significance—is placed in God's care.

"The rock of my strength, my refuge is in God."

David repeats the truth.

Because the soul often needs reminding.

"Trust in Him at all times, O people…"

This is not occasional.

Not only in moments of clarity or calm.

At all times.

"Pour out your heart before Him…"

There is openness here.

Nothing held back. Nothing managed.

Everything brought before God.

"*God is a refuge for us.*"

Not in theory.

In reality.

This Psalm shows us that trust is not only active—it is also quiet.

It is the willingness to stop striving inwardly and rest in what is already true about God.

Supporting Scriptures

- **Isaiah 30:15** — "For thus the Lord God, the Holy One of Israel, has said,

"In repentance and rest you will be saved,
In quietness and trust is your strength."
But you were not willing,"

- **Philippians 4:6–7** — "[6] Be anxious for nothing, but in everything by prayer and supplication with thanksgiving let your requests be made known to God. [7] And the peace of God, which surpasses all comprehension, will guard your hearts and your minds in Christ Jesus."
- **1 Peter 5:7** — " casting all your anxiety on Him, because He cares for you."

Personal Application

Take time to quiet your thoughts before God.

Do not rush through your concerns. Bring them fully, honestly, and then allow your heart to rest in Him.

Let your trust become steady—not driven by urgency, but grounded in truth.

Linger Thought

Quiet trust rests in God without needing to control what comes next.

Dwelling in His Shelter

Psalm 91:1–2

1 He who dwells in the shelter of the Most High
Will abide in the shadow of the Almighty.
2 I will say to the Lord, "My refuge and my fortress,
My God, in whom I trust!"

Reflection

"*He who dwells in the shelter of the Most High…*"

This is more than a moment of turning to God.

It is a place of remaining.

To dwell is to stay—to make your place there. Not visiting occasionally, not returning only in difficulty, but living in continual dependence on God.

"*In the shadow of the Almighty…*"

A shadow implies closeness.

You do not stand at a distance and remain in the shadow. You stay near. You remain under His covering.

This is not about physical location.

It is about relationship.

It is about where the heart rests.

"*I will say to the Lord, 'My refuge and my fortress…*'"

There is a declaration here.

Not just a quiet belief, but a settled statement of trust.

God is described as both refuge and fortress.

A refuge—a place of safety and rest.

A fortress—a place of strength and protection.

He is both gentle and strong.

"*My God, in whom I trust*!"

This is personal.

Not general.

Not distant.

My God.

Trust is not abstract. It is placed in someone.

And that trust is not built on changing conditions—it is built on who God is.

This Psalm does not suggest that life will be without danger.

It shows where safety is found in the midst of it.

Not in avoiding difficulty.

But in remaining close to God.

Dwelling in His presence changes how we face what comes.

Not because everything is removed.

But because we are not facing it alone.

Supporting Scriptures

- **Psalm 27:5** — "For in the day of trouble He will conceal me in His tabernacle;
In the secret place of His tent He will hide me;
He will lift me up on a rock."
- **Proverbs 18:10** — "The name of the Lord is a strong tower;
The righteous runs into it and is safe."
- **John 15:5** — "[5] I am the vine, you are the branches; he who abides in Me and I in him, he bears much fruit, for apart from Me you can do nothing."

Personal Application

Make time with God a place where you remain—not just where you return in difficulty.

Stay near in your thinking, your decisions, and your daily life.

Let your trust in Him be steady and personal.

Linger Thought

Those who stay near to God find their safety in Him.

Where Help Comes From

Psalm 121:1–2

1 I will lift up my eyes to the mountains;
From where shall my help come?
2 My help *comes* from the Lord,
Who made heaven and earth.

Reflection

"I will lift up my eyes to the mountains…"

David begins with a familiar image.

Mountains often represent strength, stability, and permanence. They rise above everything else, unmoved and enduring. It would be natural to look to them as a place of security.

But David does not stop there.

"From where shall my help come?"

He asks the question directly.

Not assuming.

Not guessing.

He considers where real help is found.

"My help comes from the Lord…"

The answer is clear.

Not from what appears strong.

Not from what seems stable.

But from God.

"*Who made heaven and earth.*"

This is why.

God is not part of creation—He is the One who made it. The mountains may appear strong, but they are not the source of help. They are part of what God has formed.

And the One who created all things is the One who sustains and provides.

David lifts his eyes—but not to remain fixed on what is seen.

He lifts them beyond that.

Because help is not found in what is visible.

It is found in the One who stands above it.

This shifts perspective.

Instead of looking around for something strong enough to hold us, we look to God—the One whose strength is not limited, whose presence is not uncertain, and whose help is not temporary.

Supporting Scriptures

- **Psalm 46:1** — "God is our refuge and

strength,
A very present help in trouble."

- **Jeremiah 17:5–7** — "[5] Thus says the Lord,

"Cursed is the man who trusts in mankind
And makes flesh his strength,
And whose heart turns away from the Lord.

[6] "For he will be like a bush in the desert
And will not see when prosperity comes,
But will live in stony wastes in the wilderness,
A land of salt without inhabitant.
[7] "Blessed is the man who trusts in the Lord
And whose trust is the Lord."

- **Hebrews 13:6** — "so that we confidently say, "The Lord is my helper, I will not be afraid. What will man do to me?"

Personal Application

Consider where you are looking for help.

Do not rely on what appears strong or stable around you. Lift your focus higher—toward God, who is the true source of help.

Return your trust to Him.

Linger Thought

True help is not found in what we see—but in the One who made it.

Unshaken

Psalm 125:1–2

1 Those who trust in the Lord
Are as Mount Zion, which cannot be moved but abides forever.
2 As the mountains surround Jerusalem,
So the Lord surrounds His people
From this time forth and forever.

Reflection

"*Those who trust in the Lord*
Are as Mount Zion, which cannot be shaken but abides forever."

Trust produces stability.

Not because circumstances stop changing—but because the foundation changes. A life that trusts in the Lord is compared to Mount Zion—firm, established, not easily moved.

Mountains do not shift with every storm.

They remain.

This is the picture David gives us—not of a life without difficulty, but of a life that is not undone by it.

"*As the mountains surround Jerusalem…*"

There is another layer here.

Jerusalem is not described as standing alone.

It is surrounded.

Protected.

Held within something greater than itself.

"*So the Lord surrounds His people…*"

This is where the image becomes personal.

God is not only the foundation beneath us—He is also the presence around us. His care is not partial. It is complete.

"*From this time forth and forever.*"

This is not temporary.

God's protection, His presence, His surrounding care—these do not come and go. They are not dependent on the moment. They extend beyond it.

This does not mean that life will be free from challenge.

But it does mean that a life anchored in God is not left exposed.

Trust in the Lord does not remove difficulty.

It removes instability.

Supporting Scriptures

- **Psalm 62:6** — "He only is my rock and my salvation,
My stronghold; I shall not be shaken."
- **Isaiah 26:4** — "Trust in the Lord forever,
For in God the Lord, *we have* an everlasting Rock."

- **Romans 8:38–39** — "[38] For I am convinced that neither death, nor life, nor angels, nor principalities, nor things present, nor things to come, nor powers, [39] nor height, nor depth, nor any other created thing, will be able to separate us from the love of God, which is in Christ Jesus our Lord."

Personal Application

Place your trust in God—not in circumstances, not in your own ability to manage what comes.

Let your confidence rest in Him, knowing that His presence surrounds you and His foundation holds you steady.

Linger Thought

A life anchored in God is not shaken by what surrounds it.

*** PRAISE & GRATITUDE ***

There is a natural place where the heart arrives when it has seen God clearly.

It responds.

Not out of obligation.

Not out of routine.

But out of recognition.

Up to this point, we have considered who God is, how we walk with Him, how we endure when life is difficult, and how we learn to trust Him. And as these truths settle, something begins to form within us.

Gratitude.

Not based on perfect circumstances, but grounded in God's unchanging character.

These Psalms guide us into that response.

They remind us to give thanks—not only when life feels steady, but because God is good.

They call us to praise—not as performance, but as a right acknowledgment of who He is.

They help us remember what we are prone to forget—His faithfulness, His provision, His enduring love.

Praise is not separate from life.

It is woven into it.

It shapes how we begin the day and how we end it. It steadies the heart. It reorients our thinking. It lifts our attention from what is temporary to what is lasting.

And it does something else:

It brings us back to God.

Not just in thought—but in response.

These reflections are an invitation to live with that awareness—to let gratitude grow, and to let praise become a natural expression of a heart that remembers.

Because when we remember who God is, giving thanks is no longer difficult.

It becomes fitting.

Joy After Weeping

Psalm 30:4–5

4 Sing praise to the Lord, you His godly ones,
And give thanks to His holy name.
5 For His anger is but for a moment,
His favor is for a lifetime;
Weeping may last for the night,
But a shout of joy *comes* in the morning.

Reflection

"*Sing praise to the Lord, you His godly ones…*"

David begins with a call.

Not to silence.

Not to reflection alone.

But to praise.

Even before the reason is fully explained.

"*And give thanks to His holy name.*"

Gratitude is not reserved only for moments when everything is clear. It is rooted in who God is—His character, His holiness, His consistent nature.

"*For His anger is but for a moment…*"

This is an important distinction.

God's correction, when it comes, is not lasting in the same way as His favor. It is measured. Purposeful. Not uncontrolled or extended beyond what is right.

"His favor is for a lifetime."

God's disposition toward His people is not marked by ongoing anger, but by enduring favor. His kindness is not brief. It remains.

"Weeping may last for the night..."

There is honesty here.

There are seasons of sorrow. Moments when grief is real, when difficulty is not easily resolved, and when the weight of life is felt deeply.

David does not dismiss that.

He acknowledges it.

But he does not leave it as the final word.

"But a shout of joy comes in the morning."

Morning does come.

Not always as quickly as we would hope. Not always in the way we expect. But sorrow is not the end of the account.

God's work continues beyond the night.

Joy is not described as something we create.

It is something that comes.

Because God is still at work.

This Psalm reminds us that while sorrow is real, it is not permanent.

God's favor remains longer than our difficulty.

Supporting Scriptures

- **Lamentations 3:22–23** —"[22]The Lord's lovingkindnesses indeed never cease, For His compassions never fail. [23] *They* are new every morning; Great is Your faithfulness."
- **John 16:20** — "Truly, truly, I say to you, that you will weep and lament, but the world will rejoice; you will grieve, but your grief will be turned into joy."
- **Isaiah 61:3** — "To grant those who mourn *in* Zion,Giving them a garland instead of ashes,The oil of gladness instead of mourning, The mantle of praise instead of a spirit of fainting. So they will be called oaks of righteousness, The planting of the Lord, that He may be glorified."

Personal Application

Do not assume that the present moment will define what comes next.

If you are in a season of difficulty, remember that it is not without limit. Continue to look to God, and trust that His work extends beyond what you currently see.

Hold steady through the night.

Linger Thought

The night may be long—but it is not the end of the story.

Give Thanks Daily

Psalm 92:1–2

1 It is good to give thanks to the Lord
And to sing praises to Your name, O Most High;
2 To declare Your lovingkindness in the morning
And Your faithfulness by night,

Reflection

"*It is good to give thanks to the Lord…*"

David begins with a simple statement.

Not complicated.

Not conditional.

Good.

Giving thanks is not merely appropriate—it is right. It aligns the heart with truth. It reminds us of what is real, even when circumstances shift.

"*And to sing praises to Your name, O Most High…*"

This is not limited to a setting or a moment. It is a response that can be carried into daily life.

"*To declare Your lovingkindness in the morning…*"

Morning marks the beginning.

A new day.

New responsibilities.

New uncertainties.

And David points us to begin there—with a declaration of God's lovingkindness. Before the day unfolds, before circumstances shape our thinking, we are reminded of who God is.

"*And Your faithfulness by night…*"

Night marks the end.

A time to reflect.

A time to consider what has passed.

And again, David directs the heart—this time to God's faithfulness. Looking back over the day, not measuring it by outcomes alone, but recognizing that God has remained steady throughout.

Morning and night.

Beginning and end.

This is a pattern.

Gratitude is not meant to be occasional. It is meant to be consistent—framing the day from start to finish.

This does not mean that every day feels easy or clear.

But it does mean that every day begins and ends with truth.

God's lovingkindness does not change with the morning.

God's faithfulness does not fade by night.

And remembering that—daily—shapes how we live.

Supporting Scriptures

- **1 Thessalonians 5:18** — "in everything give thanks; for this is God's will for you in Christ Jesus."
- **Psalm 136:1** — "Give thanks to the Lord, for He is good, For His lovingkindness is everlasting."
- **Hebrews 13:15** — "Through Him then, let us continually offer up a sacrifice of praise to God, that is, the fruit of lips that give thanks to His name."

Personal Application

Begin your day by remembering God's lovingkindness. End your day by recalling His faithfulness.

Let gratitude become a daily pattern—not dependent on circumstances, but grounded in who God is.

Linger Thought

When gratitude frames the day, truth shapes the heart.

Come and Sing

Psalm 95:1–3

1 O come, let us sing for joy to the Lord,
Let us shout joyfully to the rock of our salvation.
2 Let us come before His presence with thanksgiving,
Let us shout joyfully to Him with psalms.
3 For the Lord is a great God
And a great King above all gods,

Reflection

"*O come, let us sing for joy to the Lord…*"

This is an invitation.

Not a command given coldly, but a call to draw near. Worship is not presented as obligation alone—it is an opportunity to respond.

"*Let us shout joyfully to the rock of our salvation.*"

There is energy here.

Not restrained.

Not distant.

Joyful.

God is described as the rock—steady, reliable, unchanging. The foundation of salvation is not uncertain. It is secure.

"*Let us come before His presence with thanksgiving…*"

Worship is not only outward expression—it is an approach.

We come *before Him.*

This is relational.

Not distant acknowledgment, but intentional drawing near.

"*With joyful shouting…*"

Again, there is expression.

Worship is not meant to be silent in the sense of being withheld. It is meant to be genuine—flowing from recognition of who God is.

"*For the Lord is a great God…*"

This is the reason.

Worship is not driven by feeling alone. It is grounded in truth.

God is great.

"*And a great King above all gods.*"

His authority is unmatched. His position is not shared. He stands above all that might compete for attention or allegiance.

This Psalm reminds us that worship begins with recognition.

When we see God rightly, response follows naturally.

Joy is not something we manufacture.

It is something that grows out of understanding.

And when we come before Him with that understanding, worship becomes more than a moment.

It becomes a response to what is true.

Supporting Scriptures

- **Psalm 100:2** — "Serve the Lord with gladness; Come before Him with joyful singing."
- **Hebrews 12:28** — "Therefore, since we receive a kingdom which cannot be shaken, let us show gratitude, by which we may offer to God an acceptable service with reverence and awe;"
- **Revelation 4:11** — "Worthy are You, our Lord and our God, to receive glory and honor and power; for You created all things, and because of Your will they existed, and were created."

Personal Application

Approach God intentionally.

Do not wait for the right feeling—begin with truth. Recognize who He is, and let that shape your response.

Let your worship be both thoughtful and genuine.

Linger Thought

When we see God clearly, worship becomes a natural response.

Enter with Thanksgiving

Psalm 100

1 Shout joyfully to the Lord, all the earth.
2 Serve the Lord with gladness;
Come before Him with joyful singing.
3 Know that the Lord Himself is God;
It is He who has made us, and not we ourselves;
We are His people and the sheep of His pasture.
4 Enter His gates with thanksgiving
And His courts with praise.
Give thanks to Him, bless His name.
5 For the Lord is good;
His lovingkindness is everlasting
And His faithfulness to all generations.

Reflection

"*Shout joyfully to the Lord, all the earth.*"

The Psalm opens with a call that reaches beyond one person.

It is for all.

Worship is not limited by place, background, or circumstance. It is a response that belongs to everyone who recognizes who God is.

"*Serve the Lord with gladness…*"

Service is often thought of as duty.

But here, it is joined with gladness.

Not forced.

Not reluctant.

Glad.

"*Come before Him with joyful singing.*"

Again, the invitation is to come.

Not to stay distant.

Not to observe.

But to draw near—with a response that reflects joy.

"*Know that the Lord Himself is God…*"

This is where everything rests.

Worship is not built on emotion—it is grounded in truth.

God is God.

It is a simple statement, but it settles many things.

"*It is He who has made us, and not we ourselves…*"

We are not self-made.

We do not define our own origin or purpose.

We belong to Him.

"*We are His people and the sheep of His pasture.*"

This is both identity and care.

We are His—and He tends what is His.

"*Enter His gates with thanksgiving*
And His courts with praise."

There is a way we approach God.

Not casually.

Not carelessly.

But with gratitude.

"*Give thanks to Him, bless His name.*"

Thanksgiving is not a moment—it is a posture.

"*For the Lord is good…*"

This is the reason.

Not because circumstances always feel good.

But because God is.

"*His lovingkindness is everlasting
And His faithfulness to all generations.*"

God's character does not change.

His goodness does not fade.

His faithfulness does not end.

This Psalm is not complicated.

It is clear.

Know who God is.
Recognize what He has done.
Respond with gratitude.

And come before Him with joy.

Supporting Scriptures

- **Psalm 136:1** — "Give thanks to the Lord, for He is good, For His lovingkindness is everlasting."
- **1 Chronicles 16:34** — "O give thanks to the Lord, for *He is* good; For His lovingkindness is everlasting."

- **Hebrews 13:15** — "Through Him then, let us continually offer up a sacrifice of praise to God, that is, the fruit of lips that give thanks to His name."

Personal Application

Approach God with intention.

Let gratitude shape how you come before Him. Remember who He is and what He has done, and allow that to guide your response.

Make thanksgiving a consistent part of your life—not only in certain moments, but as a daily posture.

Linger Thought

Gratitude is the doorway through which we enter into God's presence.

Bless the Lord

Psalm 103:1–5

1 Bless the Lord, O my soul,
And all that is within me, *bless* His holy name.
2 Bless the Lord, O my soul,
And forget none of His benefits;
3 Who pardons all your iniquities,
Who heals all your diseases;
4 Who redeems your life from the pit,
Who crowns you with lovingkindness and compassion;
5 Who satisfies your years with good things,
So that your youth is renewed like the eagle.

Reflection

"*Bless the Lord, O my soul…*"

David begins by speaking to himself.

Not because he is unsure—but because he understands something important:

The heart does not always move in the right direction on its own.

So he gives it direction.

Bless the Lord.

"*And all that is within me, bless His holy name.*"

This is not partial.

Not a surface response.

All that is within me.

Every part of the inner life brought into alignment with praise.

"*Bless the Lord, O my soul,*
And forget none of His benefits…"

This is where the focus sharpens.

Do not forget.

Forgetting is easy.

Not intentionally—but gradually. What God has done can fade from attention as new concerns take its place. And when that happens, gratitude weakens.

So David reminds himself.

Remember.

"*Who pardons all your iniquities…*"

Forgiveness.

Not partial.
Not uncertain.

Complete.

"*Who heals all your diseases…*"

God's care reaches both inward and outward. His work is restorative.

"*Who redeems your life from the pit…*"

God rescues.

Not always in ways we immediately see—but in ways that are real and lasting.

"*Who crowns you with lovingkindness and compassion…*"

This is how God deals with us.

Not harshly.
Not coldly.

But with kindness and compassion that surround our lives.

"Who satisfies your years with good things…"

God provides.

Not always in excess—but in what is truly good.

"So that your youth is renewed like the eagle."

There is renewal.

Strength that returns.

Perspective that is restored.

David does not leave these truths as general statements.

He brings them close.

He speaks them to his own soul—so that his response is shaped by what is true, not by what is momentary.

Supporting Scriptures

- **Psalm 116:12** — "What shall I render to the Lord For all His benefits toward me?"
- **Ephesians 1:7** — "In Him we have redemption through His blood, the forgiveness of our trespasses, according to the riches of His grace"
- **James 1:17** — "Every good thing given and every perfect gift is from above, coming down from the Father of lights, with whom there is no variation or shifting shadow."

Personal Application

Take time to remember what God has done.

Do not allow His work in your life to fade from attention. Speak truth to your own heart. Let gratitude be shaped by remembrance.

Linger Thought

Gratitude grows when we remember what God has done.

His Lovingkindness Endures

Psalm 136:1–3

1 Give thanks to the Lord, for He is good,
For His lovingkindness is everlasting.
2 Give thanks to the God of gods,
For His lovingkindness is everlasting.
3 Give thanks to the Lord of lords,
For His lovingkindness is everlasting.

Reflection

"*Give thanks to the Lord, for He is good…*"

This is where the Psalm begins.

Not with circumstances.

Not with outcomes.

But with God's character.

He is good.

And that truth does not shift.

"*For His lovingkindness is everlasting.*"

This line is repeated throughout the Psalm.

Again and again.

Not because it is unclear—but because it is essential.

God's lovingkindness does not fade.

It does not come and go.

It does not depend on what we experience in a given moment.

It endures.

"Give thanks to the God of gods…
Give thanks to the Lord of lords…"

There is no comparison.

God stands above all. His authority is unmatched, His position unchallenged. And yet, the emphasis returns again—not first to His power, but to His enduring love.

"For His lovingkindness is everlasting."

This repetition is purposeful.

Because we are prone to forget.

When life is steady, we may not think about it. When life is difficult, we may question it.

But the truth remains the same in both.

God's lovingkindness does not change with our circumstances.

It is constant.

This Psalm invites us to anchor our gratitude not in what is happening, but in who God is.

To return, again and again, to the same truth:

He is good.
His love endures.

And that is reason enough to give thanks.

Supporting Scriptures

- **Lamentations 3:22** —

"The Lord's lovingkindnesses indeed never cease,
For His compassions never fail."

- **Psalm 100:5** — "For the Lord is good;

His lovingkindness is everlasting
And His faithfulness to all generations."

- **Romans 8:38–39** — "[38] For I am convinced that neither death, nor life, nor angels, nor principalities, nor things present, nor things to come, nor powers, [39] nor height, nor depth, nor any other created thing, will be able to separate us from the love of God, which is in Christ Jesus our Lord."

Personal Application

Return often to what does not change.

When your circumstances shift, remind yourself of God's enduring love. Let that truth shape your gratitude, even when everything else feels uncertain.

Linger Thought

God's love does not fade—it remains, steady and sure.

Let Everything Praise

Psalm 150

1 Praise the Lord!
Praise God in His sanctuary;
Praise Him in His mighty expanse.
2 Praise Him for His mighty deeds;
Praise Him according to His excellent greatness.
3 Praise Him with trumpet sound;
Praise Him with harp and lyre.
4 Praise Him with timbrel and dancing;
Praise Him with stringed instruments and pipe.
5 Praise Him with loud cymbals;
Praise Him with resounding cymbals.
6 Let everything that has breath praise the Lord.
Praise the Lord!

Reflection

"*Praise the Lord!*"

This Psalm does not begin quietly.

It begins with a declaration.

Not hesitant.

Not reserved.

Clear.

Praise is not presented as optional—it is presented as the right response to who God is.

"Praise God in His sanctuary;
Praise Him in His mighty expanse."

Praise is not limited to one place.

Not confined to a building.
Not restricted to a moment.

It extends wherever God's presence and power are recognized—which is everywhere.

"Praise Him for His mighty deeds;
Praise Him according to His excellent greatness."

There are reasons for praise.

What God has done.
Who God is.

His works and His character.

Both are worthy of response.

Then the Psalm expands further:

"Praise Him with trumpet sound…
Praise Him with harp and lyre…"

Instrument after instrument is named.

Different expressions.
Different voices.
Different ways of responding.

This is not about uniformity.

It is about fullness.

Everything that can express praise is called to do so.

"Let everything that has breath praise the Lord."

This is the conclusion.

If you have breath, you have reason.

Not based on circumstance.
Not based on condition.

But based on life itself—and the One who gives it.

Praise is not dependent on everything being resolved.

It is rooted in recognizing God.

And when that recognition is clear, praise becomes natural.

Not forced.
Not artificial.

But fitting.

Supporting Scriptures

- **Psalm 145:3** — "Great is the Lord, and highly to be praised, And His greatness is unsearchable."
- **Hebrews 13:15** — "Through Him then, let us continually offer up a sacrifice of praise to God, that is, the fruit of lips that give thanks to His name."
- **Revelation 5:13** — "And every created thing which is in heaven and on the earth and under the earth and on the sea, and all things in them, I heard saying, "To Him who sits on the throne, and to the Lamb, *be* blessing and honor and glory and dominion forever and ever."

Personal Application

Do not limit your response to God.

Let praise be part of your daily life—not only in specific moments, but as a natural response to who He is.

Use your voice. Use your attention. Use your life.

Linger Thought

If you have breath, you have reason to praise.

*** GOD'S GREATER PLAN ***

There is more taking place than what we see in front of us.

Life often feels immediate—focused on what is happening now, what needs to be resolved, what lies just ahead. But Scripture reminds us that God's work is not limited to the present moment.

It is part of a greater plan.

These Psalms lift our attention beyond daily experience and into that larger reality. They show us that God's authority is not challenged by human effort, that His purposes are not uncertain, and that His plan is not incomplete.

We see resistance—but we also see that it is ultimately in vain.

We see suffering—but we are reminded that it does not stand alone.

We see promise—but we are also shown that its fulfillment is sure.

God is not reacting to events.

He is accomplishing what He has already established.

This does not remove the weight of what we experience now.

But it places it in context.

We are not walking through isolated moments. We are living within a story that God is unfolding—one that is directed by His authority and secured by His purpose.

And because of that, we can move forward with confidence.

Not because we see everything clearly.

But because we know the One who does.

God's plan is greater than what we face today.

And it is moving forward—exactly as He has said.

The Sovereign King

Psalm 2:1–4

1 Why are the nations in an uproar
And the peoples devising a vain thing?
2 The kings of the earth take their stand
And the rulers take counsel together
Against the Lord and against His Anointed, saying,
3 "Let us tear their fetters apart
And cast away their cords from us!"
4 He who sits in the heavens laughs,
The Lord scoffs at them.

Reflection

"Why are the nations in an uproar
And the peoples devising a vain thing?"

The Psalm begins with movement.

Noise.

Planning.

Opposition.

Nations gathering. People organizing. Voices rising. All directed toward something that appears strong—human authority, human effort, human intent.

But David asks a question:

Why?

Not because he lacks understanding—but because what is happening is ultimately without foundation.

"*The kings of the earth take their stand…*
Against the Lord and against His Anointed…"

There is resistance here.

A deliberate attempt to oppose God's authority. To establish independence. To move forward without regard for Him.

"*Let us tear their fetters apart…*"

This is the desire:

To remove restraint.
To define direction apart from God.
To live without His authority.

But then the Psalm shifts perspective.

"*He who sits in the heavens laughs…*"

Not in mockery as we might think of it—but in recognition.

God is not threatened.

He is not unsettled by the plans of men. He is not reacting, adjusting, or concerned about being overcome.

He is seated.

That matters.

He is not standing in response to events. He is not moving into position. He is already in authority.

The noise below does not change the reality above.

This Psalm reminds us of something essential:

God's rule is not challenged by human effort.

No matter how organized, how determined, or how widespread opposition may appear, it does not alter who He is or what He has established.

This is not just a statement about the world.

It is a reminder for the heart.

There are moments when things around us feel unsettled—when voices are loud, when direction seems uncertain, when control appears to shift.

And in those moments, this truth remains:

God is still seated.

God is still ruling.

And His authority has not changed.

Supporting Scriptures

- **Isaiah 40:22–23** — "22 It is He who sits above the circle of the earth,
And its inhabitants are like grasshoppers,
Who stretches out the heavens like a curtain
And spreads them out like a tent to dwell in.
23 He *it is* who reduces rulers to nothing,
Who makes the judges of the earth meaningless."
- **Daniel 4:35** — "All the inhabitants of the earth are accounted as nothing,
But He does according to His will in the host of heaven
And *among* the inhabitants of earth;

And no one can ward off His hand
Or say to Him, 'What have You done?'"

- **Acts 4:25–28** — "[25] who by the Holy
Spirit, *through* the mouth of our father David Your servant,
said,

- 'Why did the Gentiles rage,
And the peoples devise futile things?
[26] 'The kings of the earth took their stand,
And the rulers were gathered together
Against the Lord and against His Christ.'

- [27] For truly in this city there were gathered
together against Your holy servant Jesus, whom You
anointed, both Herod and Pontius Pilate, along
with the Gentiles and the peoples of Israel, [28] to do
whatever Your hand and Your purpose predestined
to occur."

Personal Application

When the world around you feels unsettled or uncertain, return your focus to God's authority.

Do not measure reality by what appears strongest in the moment. Remember who is truly in control.

Let that steady your thinking.

Linger Thought

God's authority is not challenged by what rises against it—it remains.

In the Midst of Suffering

Psalm 22:1–5

1 My God, my God, why have You forsaken me?
Far from my deliverance are the words of my groaning.
2 O my God, I cry by day, but You do not answer;
And by night, but I have no rest.
3 Yet You are holy,
O You who are enthroned upon the praises of Israel.
4 In You our fathers trusted;
They trusted and You delivered them.
5 To You they cried out and were delivered;
In You they trusted and were not disappointed.

Reflection

"*My God, my God, why have You forsaken me?*"

These are some of the most direct and weighty words found in the Psalms.

They express not just difficulty—but deep distress.

A sense of distance.

A feeling of being left alone.

This is not a light moment.

It is the language of suffering.

"*Far from my deliverance are the words of my groaning…*"

The psalmist cries out—but relief does not come immediately. The words seem to fall short of the help he is seeking.

"*O my God, I cry by day, but You do not answer;
And by night, but I have no rest.*"

This is persistence without visible response.

Effort without resolution.

The kind of experience that tests not only endurance—but understanding.

And yet—

The Psalm does not stop with the question.

"*Yet You are holy…*"

This is the turning point.

Not because the situation has changed.

But because truth is brought back into view.

God's character remains steady—even when circumstances are not.

"*You who are enthroned upon the praises of Israel.*"

God is still in His rightful place.

Still reigning.

Still worthy.

"*In You our fathers trusted;
They trusted and You delivered them.*"

The psalmist looks back.

Not to escape the present, but to anchor himself in what is known. Others have trusted God—and He has proven faithful.

"*To You they cried out and were delivered…*"

This is remembrance.

"*And in You they trusted and were not disappointed.*"

This is confidence drawn from history.

This Psalm holds two realities together:

Honest suffering.

Steady truth.

The feeling of distance does not erase the reality of who God is.

And in that tension, the psalmist remains anchored—not in what he feels, but in what is true.

Supporting Scriptures

- **Matthew 27:46** — " About the ninth hour Jesus cried out with a loud voice, saying, "Eli, Eli, lama sabachthani?" that is, "My God, My God, why have You forsaken Me?"
- **Hebrews 12:2** — "fixing our eyes on Jesus, the author and perfecter of faith, who for the joy set before Him endured the cross, despising the shame, and has sat down at the right hand of the throne of God."
- **2 Corinthians 4:17–18** — "[17] For momentary, light affliction is producing for us an eternal weight of glory far beyond all comparison, [18] while we look not at the things which are seen, but at the things which are not seen; for the things which are seen are temporal, but the things which are not seen are eternal."

Personal Application

When you feel distant from God, do not assume that He has changed.

Bring your questions honestly, but return to what you know is true about Him. Let truth steady you when feelings are unsettled.

Linger Thought

Even in suffering, what is true about God does not change.

The Exalted Lord

Psalm 110:1

The Lord says to my Lord:
"Sit at My right hand
Until I make Your enemies a footstool for Your feet."

Reflection

"The Lord says to my Lord…"

David records a statement that reaches beyond his own time.

It is not merely about earthly authority. It points to something greater—someone greater.

"Sit at My right hand…"

This is a position of honor and authority.

To sit at the right hand is not to wait passively, but to be established in rule. It is a place that is given, not earned by human effort, and it reflects complete authority.

"Until I make Your enemies a footstool for Your feet."

This is a statement of certainty.

Not possibility.

Not intention.

Certainty.

God's purposes are not uncertain or incomplete. What He has declared will be accomplished. Opposition does not change the outcome—it only exists within the timeframe of what God has already determined.

This Psalm lifts our attention beyond immediate circumstances.

It reminds us that God's plan is not confined to what we see in front of us. There is a larger reality at work—one that is unfolding according to His authority and timing.

The Lord is not waiting to see what will happen.

He has already spoken.

And what He has spoken will stand.

For us, this means that our confidence is not placed in shifting events, but in God's established purpose. What may seem unresolved now is not outside of His control.

There is a direction to all things.

And it is not uncertain.

Supporting Scriptures

- **Acts 2:34–36** — "34 For it was not David who ascended into heaven, but he himself says:

'The Lord said to my Lord,
"Sit at My right hand,
35 Until I make Your enemies a footstool for
Your feet."

- **Hebrews 1:3** — "And He is the radiance of His glory and the exact representation of His nature, and upholds all things by the word of His power. When He had made purification of sins, He sat down at the right hand of the Majesty on high,"
- **1 Corinthians 15:25** — "He must reign until He has put all His enemies under His feet…"

Personal Application

Lift your perspective beyond what is immediate.

Do not measure reality only by what you see happening now. Remember that God's purposes are established and will be fulfilled.

Let that give you confidence as you move forward.

Linger Thought

God's plan is not unfolding uncertainly—it is being carried out with purpose.

Back Cover Summary

Walking Through the Psalms

A Journey of Truth, Trust, and Praise

Life does not always move in clear or predictable ways. There are moments of confidence, but also moments of uncertainty, waiting, and quiet struggle.

The Psalms speak to all of it.

This book is a collection of carefully chosen reflections drawn from the Psalms—each one focused on a small portion of Scripture and written to be read slowly and thoughtfully. Rather than covering entire chapters, each entry highlights a single truth, allowing it to settle and shape the way we think and live.

These reflections follow a simple path:

Knowing God.
Walking with God.
Facing difficulty.
Learning to trust.
Responding with praise.

And remembering that God's plan is greater than what we see.

Written in a warm and steady voice, this book is not a commentary or devotional program, but a collection of truths—intended to be returned to, reflected on, and lived out over time.

Whether read daily or revisited as needed, these reflections are meant to help steady the heart, clarify what is true, and guide a consistent walk with God.

"These are the truths I would share with my own children—one step at a time."

Appendix — The Psalms in the Life of Christ

The Book of Psalms is not only a collection of prayers, songs, and reflections—it also points forward.

Long before the events of the New Testament, the Psalms speak in ways that reach beyond their immediate setting. They express truths about God, but they also anticipate the coming of the Messiah.

When we read the life of Jesus, we find that the Psalms are not distant from His story.

They are woven into it.

Jesus quoted from the Psalms.

He lived in fulfillment of them.

And in some of His most significant moments, their words became His own.

This appendix highlights several key places where the Psalms connect directly to the life and ministry of Christ. The goal is not to provide a full study, but to help you see how these passages point to Him—and how they continue to deepen our understanding of who He is.

Psalm 2:7 — The Son Declared

"You are My Son,
Today I have begotten You."

This Psalm speaks of God's appointed King—His Son—who will rule with authority. In the New Testament, this truth is applied directly to Christ (see Acts 13:33). It affirms that Jesus is not only a teacher or prophet, but the Son of God, established in authority by the Father.

Psalm 8:4–6 — Humanity and Authority

"What is man that You take thought of him…?"

This Psalm reflects on the place of humanity in God's creation. In the New Testament (Hebrews 2:6–9), it is applied to Christ—who took on human nature and fulfilled what humanity was intended to be. Through Him, authority and purpose are restored.

Psalm 22:1 — The Suffering Savior

"My God, my God, why have You forsaken me?"

Jesus spoke these words on the cross (Matthew 27:46). Psalm 22 describes suffering in vivid detail—yet it was written long before the crucifixion. It reminds us that Christ's suffering was not unexpected. It was part of God's plan, foretold and fulfilled.

Psalm 22:16–18 — Details of the Cross

"They pierced my hands and my feet…
They divide my garments among them…"

These words closely reflect the events of the crucifixion (John 19:23–24). The Psalm provides a picture of suffering that aligns with what Christ endured, showing again that His death was not random, but purposeful.

Psalm 31:5 — Final Words of Trust

"Into Your hand I commit my spirit…"

These were among the final words of Jesus on the cross (Luke 23:46). Even in death, He entrusted Himself fully to the Father. This reflects complete trust—not only in life, but in the moment of surrender.

Psalm 34:20 — Preserved in Death

"He keeps all his bones,
Not one of them is broken."

This Psalm is reflected in the account of the crucifixion, where Jesus' bones were not broken (John 19:36). What might seem like a small detail reveals careful fulfillment of what had been written.

Psalm 41:9 — Betrayal Foretold

"Even my close friend in whom I trusted…
Has lifted up his heel against me."

Jesus applied this to His betrayal by Judas (John 13:18). The Psalm captures the pain of betrayal—something Christ experienced firsthand.

Psalm 69:9 — Zeal for God's House

"Zeal for Your house has consumed me…"

This is connected to Jesus cleansing the temple (John 2:17). His actions were not impulsive—they reflected a deep commitment to the honor of God.

Psalm 69:21 — Given Vinegar

"They also gave me gall for my food
And for my thirst they gave me vinegar to drink."

This was fulfilled during the crucifixion (Matthew 27:34). Even in suffering, the details align with what had been written.

Psalm 110:1 — Exalted Authority

"The Lord says to my Lord:
'Sit at My right hand…'"

Jesus Himself quoted this Psalm (Matthew 22:44) to reveal His authority. After His resurrection and ascension, this position is affirmed (Hebrews 1:3). He is not only the suffering Savior—He is the exalted Lord.

Closing Reflection

The Psalms are not separate from the message of the New Testament.

They prepare the way for it.

They give language to suffering, trust, and praise—and they also point forward to the One who would fulfill God's plan completely.

When we read the Psalms, we are not only reading expressions of faith.

We are seeing, in part, the life and work of Christ.

And this deepens our understanding.

Because the same God who inspired these words is the One who brought them to fulfillment—faithfully, fully, and with purpose.

Appendix — Understanding Selah

Throughout the Book of Psalms, a single word appears again and again:

Selah.

It is not translated, and its exact meaning is not fully known. But its purpose is widely understood.

It marks a pause.

Not an empty pause—but a deliberate one.

A moment to stop.
To reflect.
To consider what has just been said.

The Psalms were often sung, and Selah may have originally indicated a musical pause or interlude. But even in that setting, the purpose remains the same:

Do not rush forward.

Let the words settle.

Think carefully about what is true.

A Different Kind of Reading

We often read quickly.

Moving from one line to the next.

From one idea to another.

From beginning to end.

But the Psalms are not meant to be rushed.

They are meant to be considered.

Selah reminds us to slow down—to give attention not only to the words, but to their meaning.

Selah and This Book

In many ways, this entire book follows the pattern of Selah.

Each reflection focuses on a small portion of Scripture—not to limit what is there, but to allow it to be seen more clearly.

Instead of moving quickly through entire chapters, we pause.

We consider one truth at a time.

We allow it to settle.

The goal is not to cover more.

The goal is to understand more clearly—and to let what is true shape how we think and live.

A Simple Way to Remember

When you come across the word **Selah**, you can think of it this way:

Pause.

Reflect.

Let it settle.

Closing Thought

God's Word is not only meant to be read.

It is meant to be considered.

Selah reminds us that taking time with truth is not a delay—it is part of the process.

And often, it is in the pause that understanding begins to deepen.

Scripture Index

How to Trust Jesus as Your Savior

The most important decision any person will ever make is what they do with Jesus Christ.
Becoming a Christian is not about joining a religion, trying harder, or becoming good enough. It is about **trust** — trusting Jesus.

The Bible tells us that every one of us has fallen short of God's perfect standard. We have all sinned. That sin separates us from God, and left on its own, it leads to death — not only physical death, but eternal separation from the God who made us and loves us.

But God did not leave us there.

In His great love, God sent His Son, Jesus Christ, to do for us what we could never do for ourselves. Jesus lived a perfect life, willingly died on the cross for our sins, was buried, and rose again. His resurrection is God's assurance that sin and death have been defeated.

The Bible speaks of this love in simple and beautiful words:

"For God so loved the world, that He gave His only begotten Son, that whoever believes in Him shall not perish, but have eternal life."

— John 3:16

Becoming a Christian is not a long process — it is a moment of trust. It is the moment when you personally rely on Jesus Christ alone to save you. It is choosing, from the heart, to say something like this:

"Jesus, I know that I cannot save myself. I believe You died for me and rose again. I place my trust in You right now to forgive my sins and give me eternal life."

The words themselves are not what save you. What matters is the posture of your heart — trusting Jesus alone to save you.

That is faith. You do not need to walk an aisle, join a church, or perform good works to be saved. Salvation is God's free gift, received by faith alone.

If you have never trusted Jesus Christ, you can do so right now — wherever you are, in the quiet of your heart. The moment you place your trust in Him, God declares you forgiven, gives you eternal life, and welcomes you as His child.

And if you have already trusted Christ, keep growing. Walk with Him day by day. Read His Word. Learn to rely on His Spirit. Remember — the Christian life begins with grace, and it continues by grace.

Scripture References

🕮 Romans 3:23

"for all have sinned and fall short of the glory of God,,"

🕮 Romans 6:23

"For the wages of sin is death, but the free gift of God is eternal life in Christ Jesus our Lord

🕮 1 Peter 3:18

"For Christ also suffered once for sins, the righteous for the unrighteous, that he might bring us to God, being put to death in the flesh but made alive in the spirit,"

🕮 John 3:16

"For God so loved the world, that he gave his only Son, that whoever believes in him should not perish but have eternal life."

🕮 Romans 10:9–10, 13

9 *because, if you confess with your mouth that Jesus is Lord and believe in your heart that God raised him from the dead, you will be saved.* 10 *For with the heart one believes and is justified, and with the mouth one confesses and is saved.*

13 *For "everyone who calls on the name of the Lord will be saved."*

These verses explain the simple and wonderful truth of salvation by grace through faith in Jesus

Continue Your Journey in the Bible

If this book has helped you begin reading and understanding the Bible, there is a natural next step: Learning how to walk with God day by day.
You do not need to take everything in at once.
Simply continue—one step at a time.

Start Here — Learning to Read and Understand
How to Read and Understand the Bible
A simple, step-by-step guide designed to help you begin reading Scripture with clarity and confidence.

Next Step — Learning to Walk with God
Walking With God
Biblical Foundations for New Believers
Once you begin to understand the Bible, the next question often becomes: *How do I live this out?* Walking With God provides a clear and steady introduction to the Christian life—helping you understand what it means to grow, trust God, and take simple steps forward each day.

Build a Strong Foundation

The Bible Unlocked

A clear guide to all 66 books of the Bible, helping you understand what each book says, why it matters, and how it fits together.

Grow in Understanding

What the Bible Is Really All About

A devotional overview of the entire Bible, showing how each book fits into God's plan.

Handling God's Word with Care

A thoughtful guide to studying the Bible faithfully and carefully.

Know God More Deeply

The Attributes of God

A clear and personal look at who God is and how His character shapes our lives.

Walk Through Scripture

Walking Through the Psalms

A slow and thoughtful journey through selected Psalms, focused on truth, trust, and praise.

That You May Believe

A reflective walk through the Gospel of John, focusing on the life and purpose of Jesus.

Learn from Biblical Lives

Lives of Faith

Reflections on key people in the Bible and how God worked through their lives.

For Families and Foundations

Foundations of Faith

A clear and steady guide to core biblical truths for individuals and families.

Reflect and Remember

Remembering God's Help — Stone by Stone

A collection of Scripture-based reflections focused on God's faithfulness in daily life.

Continue reading.
Continue growing.
Continue walking with God.

About the Author

Russell Vance McFall is a lifelong student of Scripture and a writer of thoughtful, faith-centered reflections and stories. With a background in software development and many years serving in children's ministry, he has spent much of his life teaching, guiding, and encouraging others in practical, everyday faith.

He and his wife homeschooled their children for over sixteen years, where many of these reflections began—not as formal writing, but as simple truths shared in daily life. His approach to writing reflects that same desire: to communicate clearly, steadily, and in a way that can be understood and lived out.

Russell is the author of multiple books, including the *Space Cadet Richard* and *Space Cadet Legacy* series, as well as works of biblical reflection. His writing emphasizes truth, character, and the importance of a consistent walk with God.

He continues to write with the goal of passing along what he has learned—one truth at a time.

Also by Russell McFall

Ordained Path Books

Clean Science Fiction and Inspirational Writing for Thoughtful Readers

---

Contemporary Fiction and Short Stories

Stories of Community, Memory, and Hope

- **Squirrel Creek Estates — Where the Porch Lights Stay On**

The Space Cadet Richard Series

Where the Legacy Began

- **The Final Countdown**
- **The Dunes of Dinkytown**
- **The Mastermind's Maze**

The Space Cadet Legacy Series

Over 30 novels of courage, friendship, and discovery — including

- **The First Gate**
- **Welcome Back, Player**
- **Flibber's Journey Home**
- **Stronger Together**
- **Phasegate Rising**

  (New missions continuing.)

Literary Humor and Reflections

Serious Nonsense — Sanity Sold Separately

Devotional and Reflection Books

- **Remembering God's Help — Stone by Stone**
- **Attributes of God**
- **This Is My Story, This Is My Song**
- **Lives of Faith**
- **Foundations of Faith**

Russell McFall writes clean fiction and thoughtful reflections designed to uplift the heart, sharpen the mind, and remind every reader that light still wins.